The Musician's Survival Manual:
A Guide to Preventing and Treating Injuries in Instrumentalists
by
Richard Norris, M.D.

Edited by
Deborah Torch

Published by the
International Conference of Symphony and Opera Musicians
(ICSOM)

Sole Distributor

MMB MUSIC, INC.
Contemporary Arts Building
3526 Washington Avenue
Saint Louis, MO 63103-1019 USA
Phone: 314 531-9635; 800 543-3771 (USA/Canada)
Fax: 314 531-8384

THE MUSICIAN'S SURVIVAL MANUAL
A Guide to Preventing and Treating Injuries in Instrumentalists
Richard Norris, M.D.

Library of Congress Preassigned Card Number: 93-077080

ISBN: 0-918812-74-7

Sole distributor:

MMB Music, Inc.
Contemporary Arts Building
3526 Washington Avenue
Saint Louis, MO 63103-1019 USA

Phone: (314) 531-9635; (800) 543-3771 (USA/Canada)
FAX: (314) 531-8384

Cover illustration by Peggy McHugh
Desktop publishing and additional graphics by Ken Ishii

First printing: February 1993
Second printing: March 1995
Printer: Crumrine Printers, San Antonio, TX

Contents

Foreword

To the college string teacher, it is both startling and alarming how often the studies and professional development of aspiring young musicians are significantly slowed or even brought to a halt by ailments affecting their arms, shoulders, and backs.

It is therefore encouraging that in recent years the medical profession has become increasingly interested in the problems connected with playing musical instruments.

Since the study of string instruments requires many hours of practice (besides the time spent in orchestra or chamber ensembles), this trend is of great importance to our students. Much more is now known and understood about the physical factors and activities involved in the playing of string instruments. Dedicated physicians with a special interest in music and musicians indeed deserve our gratitude for the advances in the relatively new field of performing arts medicine.

An outstanding example of such a physician is Dr. Richard N. Norris. I have had the pleasure of knowing Dr. Norris for a number of years and have learned that helping young musicians is quite clearly a passion for him. His work with numerous patients, as well as his popular course given at the New England Conservatory, has brought him into contact with a great number of string players and other instrumentalists. His course on health education for musicians, a pioneer venture for a major music conservatory, was offered for credit. The curriculum included aspects of anatomical, physiological, and physical education. Dr. Norris has also been extremely successful giving talks at music festivals and other summer music programs. All of these efforts have helped young musicians achieve far greater insights into the functioning of the body in relation to musical performance.

It is of course a logical further step to deal with the prevention of physical ailments. I believe that Dr. Norris's work in this respect, too, is of the greatest importance. The preventive measures and exercises he advocates are central to his approach. One can only hope that Dr. Norris's work will find wide dissemination among musicians.

Eric Rosenblith
Chairman, String Department, New England Conservatory
Faculty, Hartt School of Music, University of Hartford

Preface

This manual is not intended to be a scholastic work. It is a collection of monographs intended to assist musicians in understanding some of the medical problems that can occur and some of the principles of prevention. Most chapters are followed by suggestions for related reading which, although not necessarily used in preparation of the chapters, offer the reader sources of further information. The redundancy in some chapters is deliberate in order to help readers who may be encountering the material for the first time.

I hope that the reader will not be offended or put off by the use of the word "patient." Lately, it has become fashionable to refer to people receiving medical or paraprofessional care as "clients." According to Webster and other dictionaries, "patient" derives from the Latin root *pati*—to suffer; suffering is the usual reason to seek medical assistance. "Client" derives from the Latin *clinare*—to lean, and refers to "a dependent; one who is under the protection of another, more powerful person." To me, the term "patient" is the more descriptive and less pejorative of the two.

Some acknowledgements are in order. My gratitude to my editor Deborah Torch and to Ken Ishii, whose devoted and painstaking attention to text and graphics made this work possible; to ICSOM chairperson Brad Buckley for his support of this project; to music medicine doctors extraordinaire Bob Sataloff, Bob Markison, Hunter Fry, and Frank Wilson, for inspiring me; and to music educators Peter Row, Victor Rosenbaum, Tom Mastroianni, Janet Horvath, and Phyllis Curtin for their support of my efforts in promoting health education among musicians.

I wish to dedicate this book to my parents, Sidney and Priscilla Norris, both health educators and music lovers; to my artistic and musical wife, Laura, for her support and assistance with this manuscript; and to the musical artists, past, present, and future, who have so enriched all of our lives.

Richard Norris

Chapter 1

Overuse Injuries: Recognition and Prevention

*No sort of exercise is so healthful or harmless that it does
not cause serious disorders, that is, when overdone.*
—*Dr. Bernardino Ramazzini (1713)*

Overuse injuries are, unfortunately, all too common among
instrumentalists. Fortunately, however, such injuries are largely
preventable and can often be treated through a combination of
proper care and a change in the habits or activities that caused
them. All musicians, from casual players to seasoned performers,
should learn how to prevent overuse injuries and how to recog-
nize the earliest possible signs of such injuries.

What is an overuse injury? It is a condition that occurs when
any biological tissue—muscle, bone, tendon, ligament, etc.—is
stressed beyond its physical limit. This can result in microtrauma
to the body part—that is, microscopic tears which lead to small
amounts of bleeding and swelling within the injured area. Some
studies (Fry) have revealed specific pathology. While runners and
dancers frequently sustain stress or fatigue fractures, musicians
more commonly develop "tendinitis." Often, the painful part is
not the tendon itself, but the muscle that is attached to the tendon.
Thus, I use the word *tendinitis* to refer to injury of the muscle-
tendon unit.

Overuse injuries can be classified as *acute* or *chronic*. An
acute overuse injury occurs following a specific incident of
stressing the tissue beyond its limits. An example would be a
musician who learns a new phrase or trill and is determined to
master it before going to bed that evening. He or she practices it
for three or four hours, and then wakes up the next day with a stiff
and painful hand or arm. Chronic overuse injury takes place more
insidiously over a longer period of time. This tendinitis starts out

as a very mild discomfort that becomes progressively severe over the course of weeks or months.

Predisposing Factors

There are at least twelve general factors that predispose a musician to suffer from overuse injuries:

1. Inadequate physical conditioning

Muscles that are tight, weak, and inadequately conditioned are more susceptible to overuse injuries than muscles that are strong and flexible. (Physical conditioning for musicians will be addressed in chapter 13.) Physical education in music schools and conservatories has been sorely neglected in the past, but awareness of its importance is slowly increasing.

2. Sudden increase in the amount of playing time

An abrupt increase in playing time is perhaps the most common cause of overuse injuries. Injuries often occur during summer music camps when a student who has been playing three or four hours per day suddenly starts to play seven or eight hours per day. Preparing for recitals or juries, or taking extra gigs during a holiday season, can also lead to overuse injuries.

3. Errors in practice habits

Musicians should learn to regard playing an instrument as a physical activity. When asked about warmup habits, musicians often report that they don't warm up at all, or consider simply playing scales or a few slow pieces to be an adequate warmup. We play a musical instrument with the entire body. At the very least, a good warmup that includes the neck, arms, shoulders, and upper and lower back is important in preventing overuse injuries. Exercises might include slow rolling of the head, slow shoulder shrugs and rolls, side bends, and torso twists. In general, practice sessions should be limited to about forty-five minutes, with a break of no less than five minutes to relax and shake out muscles. (One may continue to practice for several hours in this fashion.) Difficult passages or those that require awkward fingering should be practiced in short segments of not more than five minutes each. The musician should then move on to other material for a while before returning to the difficult segment. When a period of increased practice or performance intensity looms on the horizon, the best way to avoid overuse injuries is to increase practice time gradually over a few weeks.

4. Errors of technique

One of the most common technical errors is playing with excessive tension, which causes the muscles to work extra hard. This is particularly common in string players' left hands when playing *forte*. Despite the increase in bow pressure, the left hand should not have to press down much harder than when playing *piano*. Often, the player is not aware of this. Pressing down even twenty to thirty per cent harder than necessary on the strings may have a cumulative effect, resulting in a gradual, progressive overuse injury. Tendinitis in the left forearm, particularly of the extensor muscles (along the back of the forearm), is the most common injury I see among violinists and violists in my medical practice. Drumsticks, horns, etc., are commonly gripped harder than necessary, as are steering wheels, pens, and telephones!

Problems with excessive tension in muscle force also occur in the neck and left shoulder in violinists, often due to inadequate or improperly fitted chin rests and shoulder rests.

Modern scientific techniques—such as motion analysis, which has been used to evaluate the technique of professional and Olympic athletes—may also become widely available in the music field, leading to a better understanding of bowing and fingering techniques. Motion analysis, along with studies of the muscles involved in actions such as vibrato, is already available in some performing arts medicine centers.

5. Change in instrument

Switching from violin to viola, from electric bass guitar to string bass, or to a piano with stiffer action can all predispose to overuse injuries. Whenever there is a change in instrument, including upgrading to a better instrument, the musician should back off slightly from a normal practice schedule, and build up again over the course of a week or two. The same is true when changing repertoire or teachers.

6. Inadequate rehabilitation of previous injuries

An important factor that is often overlooked is prior injury. The tendinitis, muscle sprain, or neck problem that has not completely resolved, but has been treated or rested just enough so that the person is able to resume playing, is likely to flare up with any additional stress. It is important to pursue therapy until the player is completely free of pain, has a full range of motion, and has fully regained endurance, strength, and coordination.

7. Improper body mechanics and posture

Disciplines such as yoga, the Alexander Technique, and Feldenkrais body-work are very important in correcting slumped posture or other poor body mechanics that increase the risk of injury, particularly to the neck and back. Proper posture is also important in carrying instruments. Of course, the heavier the instrument, the more problems it presents, especially for a smaller person. In general, it is best not to carry a heavy instrument with only one hand or hang it from one shoulder, as this creates undue strain on the shoulder and back. A better way is to use a strap that is long enough to go over the head and across the chest in order to distribute the weight of the instrument evenly. For heavier instruments, there are backpacks or gig bags available. Wheels on the bottom of the case will help cellists and bassists. When lifting and carrying heavier stringed instruments, it is important to observe proper body mechanics, such as bending from the knees and keeping loads close to the body (see chapters 5 and 6).

8. Stressful nonmusical activities

Refinishing furniture, pulling weeds, typing, knitting, or needlework can all result in tendinitis-like overuse problems. As with playing an instrument, these injuries can be avoided by awareness, frequent rests, and gradual increases in the duration and intensity of the activity.

9. Anatomical variations

Musicians, especially string players, may experience problems resulting from anatomical anomalies exacerbated by the demands of a particular instrument. Examples are thoracic outlet syndrome (nerve or blood vessel compression at the base of the neck from an extra cervical rib), increased joint laxity, or abnormal tendon connections or insertions (see chapter 11).

10. Gender

Studies indicate that young women seem most at risk for overuse injuries (Fishbein and Middlestadt). The reasons are not clear; because men are less likely to seek health care, perhaps women are disproportionately represented in the statistics. Women's muscles are often smaller, and may therefore be more susceptible to overuse. This theory is supported by the fact that in the Fishbein and Middlestadt study, incidence of injury rises with increasing size of instrument. In my own practice, the majority of injured double-bass players I have seen were females, even though they constitute only a small proportion of all bassists. These findings should not discourage smaller persons from playing large instruments, but may indicate an increased need for awareness, good physical conditioning, and good practice habits.

11. Quality of instrument

A wind instrument with leaky valves or pads, a string instrument with a bridge or nut that is too high, or a piano that "speaks" poorly in the middle register necessitates extra or excessive force on the part of the player, with increased risk of injury.

12. Environmental factors

Inadequate lighting or poorly copied parts can cause eyestrain, but probably the most bothersome environmental factor is cold temperature. Playing evening concerts at outdoor music festivals in the Rockies or Berkshires towards the end of the summer or playing in stone cathedrals in midwinter can be chilling experiences! At low temperatures, nerve conduction slows, making it harder for the fingers to respond quickly. In addition, the fluid in the joints thickens, diminishing the sensitivity of the fingers. In this situation, the player needs to make sure he or she warms up adequately prior to play—a real physical warmup, not just scales. Appropriate dress is also important. Long sleeves and a high neckline may not be as stylish as a strapless gown for a female soloist, but may help avoid frozen hands. It may be necessary to wear long johns under a tux, or even thin, fingerless gloves if playing in a pit.

Symptoms

How do you know if you have developed an overuse injury? The most common indicator is pain or discomfort. Overuse injuries are graded into five categories (Fry):

1. pain at one site only, and only while playing;
2. pain at multiple sites;
3. pain that persists well beyond the time when the musician stops playing, along with some loss of coordination;
4. all of the above; in addition, many activities of daily living (ADLs) begin to cause pain;
5. all of the above, but all daily activities that engage the affected body part cause pain.

Most overuse injuries fall into grades 1, 2, or 3. The earlier the symptoms are recognized and treated, the sooner and more completely recovery occurs. In the earliest stages, overuse injuries may be experienced as stiffness without significant amounts of pain.

Nerve Compression

Numbness and tingling, the feeling of "pins and needles," or electric shock sensations are usually indicative of nerve compression. This occurs most commonly at the wrist as carpal tunnel syndrome (CTS), which usually causes numbness and tingling in the thumb, index, and middle fingers. CTS can be associated with a flexed wrist position, such as when playing in tenth position or above on the violin or viola. Practicing in the higher positions for only short periods of time, if possible, will avoid irritating the nerve at the wrist.

Nerve compression in the index finger is common in flutists (left hand), bass players who use a French-style bow grip, and mallet players. This problem is often misdiagnosed as CTS by physicians unfamiliar with musicians' injuries (see chapter 8).

Compression of the ulnar nerve, which lies in the groove on the inside of the elbow (the "funny bone"), is called cubital tunnel syndrome (see chapter 7). When the elbow is bent (flexed), the canal of the cubital tunnel narrows and the nerve is stretched at the same time. The left elbow of the cellist (in the first few positions) and the right elbow of the piccolo player are particularly vulnerable due to the maximally flexed position. In the "chin strings," the rotated (supinated) and flexed position of the left arm, especially in the higher positions, also stresses the ulnar nerve at the elbow. One other factor for increased risk in string players is that the flexor carpi ulnaris muscles, which align the wrist to play in the higher positions on violin or viola, surround the ulnar nerve at the elbow. When these muscles are working and contracting, they cause additional compression on the ulnar nerve.

Besides pain in the elbow region, symptoms of cubital tunnel syndrome include numbness and tingling in the fourth and fifth fingers of the hand, where the ulnar nerve ends; loss of coordination; and, in severe cases, muscle wasting (atrophy).

Nerves can also be compressed in the neck or thoracic outlet region (see chapter 4), producing similar symptoms in the hand. Electrodiagnostic testing can help pinpoint the sources of nerve compression problems.

Treatment

Perhaps the most important treatment is rest. We all know how difficult it is for professional musicians to take time off to rest, so we must borrow the concept of *relative* rest from sports medicine. Depending on the severity of the injury, this may mean cutting back, rather than completely stopping, practice and performances. For students, there is less justification for not markedly cutting back or stopping for a brief period of time when necessary. It is better to postpone a jury or an audition than to allow an injury to worsen.

During the period of relative rest, technique should be assessed by a professional, looking especially for areas of excessive tension or stress. If these are deemed significant factors by either the teacher or the physician, the musician would do well to consider a stress management program that includes biofeedback training. Biofeedback can be used for both general muscle relaxation and for playing an instrument, so one can learn to relax the specific muscle groups that may be overworking. Video feedback—watching oneself on a video monitor while working with a posture or movement specialist—is an effective tool; a permanent tape of the session can be made for further review. Alexander or Feldenkrais lessons are often helpful.

Easy stretching exercises to maintain length and movement in injured muscles and tendons are also important (see chapter 2), and should be preceded by gentle warmth to help relax the affected part. Stretching should be done only to the point of mild discomfort. As pain from the injury subsides, gentle strengthening exercises may be instituted. Although it is preferable to do these exercises under the supervision of an occupational or physical therapist, very judicious patients may continue at home. When the muscles being strengthened are small, it is better to proceed slowly and with caution than to risk reinjury. With forearm muscle overuse, special attention should be paid to strengthening muscles of the upper arms, chest, and trunk.

Thermotherapy in the form of ice massage and gentle heat is often effective. Heat should be applied before stretching and strengthening, with ice used afterward for five to ten minutes. Ice, rather than heat, should be used in acutely inflamed (hot) conditions. Anti-inflammatory medications such as Motrin, ibuprofen, aspirin, Indocin, and others may be used, but should never be the primary treatment. Persons with a history of bleeding or stomach ulcers should be especially cautious when using these medications.

Activities of Daily Living

One of the most commonly overlooked reasons for treatment failure in what might appear to be an adequate therapy program is the effect of activities of daily living (ADLs). When musicians complain of pain that accompanies ordinary activities such as brushing hair or teeth, opening doorknobs and the like, coupled with inability to play for a number of weeks, I always refer them for a session or two with an occupational therapist. During these sessions, ADLs are evaluated and modified, and adaptive equipment is introduced if necessary. For people with severe arthritis, there are many adaptive devices that make ADLs easier on the arms and hands. These devices include built-up foam handles for eating utensils, writing utensils, hairbrushes, and razors. Levers attached to doorknobs ease opening. Jar wrenches remove lids without force; keyholders prevent pinching the key between the thumb and index finger when opening doors.

As driving can be very hard on the arms, particularly in a car without power steering or automatic transmission, one should drive as little as possible during recuperation. Musicians should avoid second jobs that require hand-intensive activities such as computer terminal operation, typing, waiting on tables, etc. Normal daily activities may be resumed gradually as symptoms subside. Meticulous attention to minimizing or eliminating the stress of daily activities on the hand and arms can make the difference between success and failure in the treatment of overuse injuries.

Surgery or cortisone injections are rarely indicated. However, conditions such as carpal tunnel syndrome or tendinitis at the base of the thumb (de Quervain's disease) often respond well to injection or surgery when conservative treatment has been unsuccessful.

Splinting to rest the injured part is often helpful, particularly when the injury is in the dominant hand. A right-handed person with tendinitis of the right arm often has trouble remembering to use the left hand instead. To prevent use of the injured hand, the splint should come all the way out to the tips of the fingers (full-length resting splint). Care must be taken not to provoke injury in the opposite arm by the added, unaccustomed use of that side. Removing the splint several times a day to do gentle movements and muscle contractions will prevent stiffness and soreness of the splinted part. Splints custom-molded by an occupational therapist will provide maximum comfort and optimal fit. Slings should be avoided, if possible, as there is some risk of ulnar nerve compression from prolonged elbow flexion.

Summary

The overuse injury that can be the bane of a student or professional musician can often be prevented or treated successfully in its early stages by increased awareness and recognition of the problem. Prevention, as always, remains the best medicine.

Suggested Reading

Bird H. Overuse injuries in musicians. *British Medical Journal* 1989 Apr 29; 298(6681): 1129-30.

Fry HJH. The effect of overuse on the musician's technique: a comparative and historical review. *International Journal of Arts Medicine* 1991 Fall; 1(1): 46-55.

Fry HJH. How to treat overuse injury: medicine for your practice. *Music Educators Journal* 1986 May; 72(9): 46-49.

Fry HJH. Patterns of overuse seen in 658 affected instrumental musicians. *International Journal of Music Education* 1988; 11: 3-16.

Fry HJH. Prevalence of overuse (injury) syndrome in Australian music schools. *British Journal of Industrial Medicine* 1987 Jan; 44(1): 35-40.

Fry HJH. Treatment of overuse syndrome in musicians: results in 175 patients. *Journal of the Royal Society of Medicine* 1988 Oct; 81(10): 572-75.

Goodman G; Staz S. Occupational therapy for musicians with upper extremity overuse syndrome: patient perceptions regarding effectiveness of treatment. *Medical Problems of Performing Artists* 1989 Mar; 4(1): 9-14.

Lederman RJ; Calabrese LH. Overuse syndromes in instrumentalists. *Medical Problems of Performing Artists* 1986 Mar; 1(1): 7-11.

Lockwood AH; Linsday ML. Reflex sympathetic dystrophy after overuse: the possible relationship to focal dystonia. *Medical Problems of Performing Artists* 1989 Sep; 4(3): 114-17.

Newmark J; Lederman RJ. Practice doesn't necessarily make perfect: incidence of overuse syndromes in amateur instrumentalists. *Medical Problems of Performing Artists* 1987 Dec; 2(4): 142-44.

Chapter 2

Nonsurgical Treatment Of Upper Extremity Disorders In Instrumentalists

Fortunately, most upper extremity injuries of musicians respond to conservative treatment. At our arts medicine center, fewer than five per cent of injuries require surgical referral and evaluation; of these, fewer than half actually receive a surgical procedure. The most common reason for surgical referral is nerve entrapment.

Nerve Entrapments

The common compressions or entrapment neuropathies occur at the carpal tunnel, cubital tunnel, and thoracic outlet. Ulnar nerve entrapment at the wrist (Guyon's canal), pronator teres syndrome, radial sensory branch neuropathy, and neurogenic thoracic outlet syndrome are relatively uncommon.

Carpal tunnel syndrome has multiple etiologies, including pregnancy, amyloid disease, and underlying diabetes. However, this discussion will be limited to occupational carpal tunnel syndrome. Gelberman has shown marked increase in carpal tunnel pressures with extremes of both flexion and extension of the wrist. This often relates directly to musical technique. Therefore, one of the first considerations in treating carpal tunnel syndrome is markedly reducing playing time, or at least avoiding positions that require sustained or repetitive flexion or extension of the wrist. Electrodiagnosis is often extremely useful in assessing both the site of the entrapment and the severity and prognosis.

The mainstay of conservative treatment for carpal tunnel syndrome is splinting, and, as was mentioned, avoiding offending activities. The splint should put the wrist in the functional position, allowing 0° to 5° of extension, leaving the fingers free. Depending on the severity of the symptoms and clinical findings, the splint may be worn only at night or throughout most of the of the day as well. The splint should be taken off several times a day for the musician to do gentle pain-free, range-of-motion exercises. Oral anti-inflammatory agents may be helpful, as may injection of a steroid preparation mixed with a local anesthetic. It is my personal preference to use soluble steroids, rather than Depo or long-acting steroids, because hand surgeons have found steroid crystals in the carpal tunnel weeks to months after an injection with Depo steroids. These crystals may eventually be mechanically irritating.

If conservative treatment is unsuccessful after a period of three to four weeks, and/or an electromyelogram (EMG) shows signs of muscle denervation, surgical referral is indicated. There is also some evidence, although inconclusive, that vitamin B_6 may be therapeutic.

Cubital tunnel syndrome may be more prevalent in string players, particularly cellists and violinists, due to the nearly continuous extremes of elbow flexion in the left arm when playing those instruments. The cubital tunnel is located on the inner aspect of the elbow; thus, when the elbow is flexed, the ulnar nerve is stretched around the elbow, and the cubital tunnel is narrowed. Both factors are potential causes of irritation of the ulnar nerve within this region. For violinists, an additional risk factor is that the ulnar nerve is surrounded by the two heads of the flexor carpi ulnaris muscle—the very muscle used to play in higher positions on the violin. The floor of the cubital tunnel is formed by the flexor sublimus muscle, which is strongly con-tracted in playing both violin and cello.

Treatment for cubital tunnel syndrome consists of splinting the elbow in extension, although not necessarily with a rigid splint: a hinge splint that allows not more than 90° of elbow flexion is best. Again, if there are signs of denervation, or if symptoms either worsen or fail to resolve within about a month, surgical consultation is indicated.

Tendinitis

Of all the upper extremity disorders in instrumentalists, pain syndromes of the muscle-tendon unit seem to be the most common. A multitude of treatment options have been found to be beneficial. The first and most important is *relative* rest. As in sports medicine, a goal of performing arts medicine is to try to keep patients playing, to the extent possible. Often, it is not necessary to cease playing, but simply to reduce and modify the playing schedule. This may take a bit of experimentation, but certainly the patient should be instructed to avoid playing to an extent that aggravates the injury. The threshold may vary from a few minutes to a few hours per day. If any amount of playing causes pain or aggravation of symptoms, then the rest should be as complete as possible. Once symptoms have abated, it is imperative that the return to playing be gradual. *Relative* rest really means avoiding pain-producing activities.

In its extreme form, rest may include immobilization, which is certainly not a benign treatment. Muscles need to contract and relax periodically, while joints depend on motion for cartilage nourishment. Perhaps the chief indicator for immobilization is pain on use of the hand in any daily activities, especially when the patient seems unable to stop using an injured dominant hand in activities of daily living. A full-length resting splint often is required to preclude hand use. Removing the splint several times a day to perform gentle pain-free, range-of-motion exercises will prevent stiffness and worsening of symptoms.

Return to Playing

Returning too rapidly to prior levels of practice and performance is one of the most common pitfalls of the rehabilitation process. A written, individualized training schedule is very helpful in giving the performer guidelines to follow (see chapter 14). Generally, in the initial stages, practice periods should be brief and rest periods long. As the injury heals, practice periods can grow progressively longer and rest periods shorter, and the patient can go from playing slow tempos and easy material to faster tempos and harder material. Sudden increases in performance time must be avoided.

Daily Activities

Modification of activities of daily living (ADLs), sometimes using adaptive equipment, is of the utmost importance in treating overuse injuries. ADLs are frequently overlooked by both the physician and patient as a source of continued aggravation to the injury and failure to improve, despite a seemingly adequate therapy program.

Modification of Posture and Technique

The role that posture, body mechanics, and faulty musical technique play in causing and perpetuating an injury must be assessed by the physician and therapist in conjunction with a music teacher. Posture away from the instrument—while working at a desk, for example—may be contributing to strain and must be addressed.

Instrument modification is often essential in both prevention and treatment of injuries—particularly hand injuries. In woodwinds, the keys are set in a "one-size-fits-all" arrangement that does not account for extreme variations in hand size and morphology (structure).

Medications

The most commonly used medications are nonsteroidal anti-inflammatory agents. Patients with a history of ulcers or bleeding disorders must be cautious when using these medications, which should be taken only after a full meal. In general, anti-inflammatory medications tend to be more useful in acute than chronic situations, and should probably not be used for more than three or four weeks at a time. Anti-inflammatory medications should rarely be used as the sole treatment, but may be helpful in conjunction with other modalities.

Injections

Injections are usually done with a solution of steroid and anesthetic. I most often use injection for de Quervain's disease: tendinitis at the base of the thumb, running in the first dorsal extensor compartment. Treatment should also include the thumb spica splint and physical modalities (see below). I may repeat an injection after a few weeks, but if the second injection does not help, surgery is indicated. Carpal tunnel syndrome and lateral epicondylitis ("tennis elbow") are often responsive to steroid injection. In my experience, true lateral epicondylitis is relatively rare in musicians, compared to the more common diffuse extensor forearm muscle pain. As a diffuse condition, forearm muscle pain does not respond to injection. Trigger finger also occasionally improves with steroid injection, which should be combined with specialized splinting and an exercise program. If there is no response to conservative treatment within three or four weeks, surgery is indicated.

Orthotics

An orthotic is a medical device, such as a splint or strap, applied to or around a bodily segment in the care of physical impairment or disability. There are numerous uses of orthotics in the treatment of upper extremity limb disorders. Orthotics can be applied to an instrument such as the flute to help stabilize it and to lessen the amount of hand force required to control it; the thumb rest on a clarinet, oboe, or flute can be modified to lessen strain.

Thermotherapy

Thermotherapy can take the form of either heat or cold. Heat is commonly applied as either a hot pack, which does not have much depth penetration, or as ultrasound, which has much deeper penetration. Ultrasound can be pulsed or continuous. Pulsed ultrasound helps to prevent excessive heat buildup and should be used in bony areas. Applying ultrasound underwater, as was commonly done in the past for small bony areas, has not proved very effective at raising tissue temperature. An ultrasound unit with a very small head works better for bony areas such as hands and wrists. In treating areas of nerve compression, ultrasound should be used only in very low doses. A normal dose, which is 1.5 to 2.0 watts/cm^2, actually has been shown to be deleterious to nerve healing. Low-dose ultrasound would be in the range of 0.5 watts/cm^2.

Fluidotherapy

Fluidotherapy uses pulverized organic material such as walnut shells or grain husks. Advantages include the ability to attain higher specific heat than with other methods of application, and the opportunity for the therapist to put his or her hands into the fluidotherapy bath to perform joint mobilization or soft-tissue massage concurrently. Although paraffin baths do not heat deep within the tissue, they are very good for dry skin and for relaxing contracted areas.

Electrical Stimulation

The use of electrical stimulation is often beneficial when there is edema or swelling, as the current can help to polarize and drive the interstitial edema (fluid between the cells) back into the vascular system. This treatment should be combined with compression and elevation. Electrical stimulation often induces gentle, rhythmic muscle contractions in sore areas, helping to relieve discomfort by removing interstitial edema and increasing blood flow to the muscle. Electrical stimulation can also be used with active muscle contraction to strengthen weak or atrophied muscles. Caution must be used with patients who have pacemakers and those with very sensitive skin, which can be irritated by the electrodes.

Massage

Massage is useful in stimulating blood flow, reducing edema, and breaking up localized areas of muscle spasm known as trigger points. Massage is also helpful for general relaxation and reduction of overall tension.

Therapeutic Exercise

Therapeutic exercise is useful both in preventing and treating specific ailments. Often, after a period of injury, the muscles in the hand and forearm become weak from disuse or nerve compression. Therapeutic exercise, along with a gradual return to playing, is necessary to restore muscle strength and endurance. Working on proximal strength greatly benefits the instrumentalist, particularly the smaller person who plays a large instrument. One area of interest to me (which, to my knowledge has not been researched) is preventive strengthening of the wrist and finger extensors, a common area for pain and dysfunction. Hand exercises must be undertaken with caution and supervision because of the risk of overdoing the exercises and thereby worsening the condition. One of the chief offenders in causing further injury is therapy putty, particularly the pink putty, which tends to be rather stiff, especially when cold. There are several different colors of putty available in varying degrees of stiffness and resistance. If putty is used, it must be used in a graded fashion. Rubber bands and manual resistance may also be used. In my opinion, a good therapeutic exercise program should address not only strength and endurance, but also flexibility and gracefulness, since these are often characteristic of fine players showing a high degree of coordination and efficiency of movement. (Further information about therapeutic exercise may be found in chapter 13.)

Feedback Techniques

Video feedback may be quite useful in treatment by allowing patients more insight into technical errors. Locating the video monitor in front of the musician and the camera to the side or rear allows the player to see his or her posture from various angles while playing; this can be done in conjunction with a physical or postural therapist, with the session recorded for later analysis. Videotaping also allows rapid or difficult passages to be played back in slow motion to assess technical errors that might otherwise be difficult to spot.

Biofeedback and a stress management program can be extremely useful in the treatment of upper extremity disorders by bringing about an overall decrease in stress and muscle tension. In my experience, one of the most common technical errors is the use of too much force in pressing on strings, keys, valves, and the like. The use of biofeedback on specific muscle groups can give the patient valuable information regarding the level of force required to perform a given task. I prefer visual biofeedback in which the data is seen on a monitor while the musician is playing, as it is difficult for a performer to concentrate simultaneously on the sound of the instrument and the sound of an aural biofeedback machine.

Summary

The bad news regarding musicians' injuries is how common they are; the good news is that the vast majority of them will respond to nonsurgical treatment. However, nonsurgical treatment is not always the conservative path—there are many conditions that respond quickly and reliably to surgical procedures. In situations of prolonged pain and disability, nonsurgical procedures should not be pursued indefinitely when surgery would correct the situation and allow the performer a rapid return to playing.

References

Baker, L. Applications of high and low voltage electrotherapeutic currents. In: *Electrotherapy.* Wolf SL,ed. New York: Churchill, Livingstone, 1981.

Eisen, A. The cubital tunnel syndrome. *Neurology* 1974 July; 24: 608-13.

Gelberman, R. The carpal tunnel syndrome: a study of carpal canal pressures. *Journal of Bone and Joint Surgery* 1981 Mar; 63-A(3): 380-83.

Gersten, JW: Effective ultrasound on tensor extensibility. *American Journal of Physical Medicine* 1955; 34: 662.

Gleck and Salliba. Application of modalities in overuse syndromes. In: *Clinics in Sports Medicine* 1987 April; 6(2): 427-64.

Griffen, JE. Physiological effects of ultrasound as it is used clinically. *Journal of American Physical Therapy* 1966 46: 18.

Hunter-Griffin, ed. Overuse injuries. In: *Clinics in Sports Medicine* 1987 April; 6(2): 225-470.

Killian, C. *High Frequency and High Voltage Protocols.* Minneapolis: Medtronic, 1984.

Lehmann, JF. Selective heating effects of ultrasound in human beings. *Archives of Physical Medicine* 1966; 47: 331-39.

Primer, C. Compression neuropathies in the upper extremity. *Orthopedic Review* 1987 June; 16(6): 463-65.

Ziskin MC. Therapeutic ultrasound. In: Michlovitz, ed. *Thermal Agents in Rehabilitation.* Philadelphia: F.A. Davis, 1986.

Chapter 3

Problems in the Neck Region, or
When Making Music is a Pain in the Neck!

There are several factors that cause neck pain in string players. First, the "chin strings" (violin and viola) can be rather "user-unfriendly" to the neck. These instruments usually require the head to be tilted and/or rotated somewhat, which can strain the muscles of the neck region, including the trapezius and levator muscles that hike the shoulder. It is difficult to avoid hiking the shoulder and tilting the head while playing, especially for players with long necks. One factor may be inadequate height of the chin rest. Most chin rests seem to have been made to fit the fiddle, not the fiddler! If the combined height of the instrument, chin rest, and shoulder rest is insufficient, the only way to secure the instrument is to hike the shoulder and tilt the head. Raising the height of the chin rest helps to correct this situation, just as clamping adaptive devices onto a telephone receiver facilitates holding the phone without hiking the shoulder. Raising the instrument from the shoulder rest would not be desirable, as this would elevate the entire instrument and create increased strain on the bow arm (see chapter 6). The chin rest can be raised by inserting cork shims under its base until the desired height is reached, or by fashioning a new rest. A raised rest that is too high to fit into the case can easily be slipped on and off by creating a dovetail joint at the base of the chin rest. Additionally, chin and shoulder rests can be adjusted or custom-molded to fit the individual, thereby avoiding the concentration of pressure responsible for the "practice mark" and concomitant skin and TMJ (jaw joint) problems.

Of course, altering the chin and shoulder rests is not the only solution to the problem of neck strain. Even with properly fitted chin and shoulder rests, one must attend to the muscles themselves, both for treatment and, more importantly, prevention of problems. We know from sports medicine that muscles that are strong and flexible are more resistant to injury than those that are tight and weak. Although it has not been documented scientifically, experience and common sense have convinced me of the benefit musicians derive from therapeutic exercise, especially to counteract unnatural positions assumed at the instrument. Gentle stretching and range-of-motion exercises are particularly important for the "chin string" players, who tilt or rotate their heads. Over months and years, such asymmetrical posture can result in muscle imbalance, with the muscles on the left side becoming shorter and stronger than those on the right. Muscle imbalance can lead to joint dysfunction and so on.

Ideally, the exercises should be preceded by the application of heat, such as a hot shower or sauna. Gentle strengthening exercises can be accomplished easily by manual resistance against the head in varying positions for seven or eight seconds at a time (see chapter 13).

Practice habits that help prevent neck disorders include limbering up the neck and shoulders with warmup exercises, and taking frequent breaks—perhaps two or three minutes at the half hour, and five or ten at the hour. Taking breaks is particularly important for youth symphonies, when the students often have orchestra rehearsal at the end of a long day of lessons, sectionals, or chamber groups.

Another culprit leading to neck disorders is the use of excessive muscular tension in securing the instrument between the chin and shoulder. In *The Compleat Violinist,* Yehudi Menuhin states that the violin should be held like a bridge, supported at both ends, not clamped at one end like a diving board. Of course, during position shifts, one must momentarily increase the proximal support to free up the left hand, but must ask oneself: "What is the least amount of force required to support the instrument?" Unfortunately, in our stressed-out world, emotional tension usually translates into muscular tension, most often in the trapezius muscles, located between the shoulder and neck. In a primordial manner, we try to protect our vulnerable necks from danger!

Muscular tension in a trapezius already overworked by a short chin rest often results in muscle spasm; in fact, chronic pain and spasm in the left trapezius and neck muscles is one of the problems most commonly encountered in players of the "chin strings." Instrumentalists, particularly pianists, often tense and hike their shoulders in response to intense musical passages. Biofeedback and relaxation/imagery exercises, along with previously mentioned therapies such as video feedback, can help to prevent excessive tension in this area. Biofeedback ideally should be done using a machine with a video display that gives visual, moment-to-moment information regarding the amount of tension in a particular muscle. Visual feedback is superior to the more common auditory system due to the difficulty of listening simultaneously to one's playing and to the signals of the machine.

Neck strain in cellists and pianists may be caused by sitting with the head positioned in front of the neck, thus increasing the work of the muscles at the back of the neck to prevent the head from falling forward. Faulty positioning, in turn, is often related to the flattening of the low back (see chapter 5), which causes the head to project forward. Also, failing to use corrective lenses when needed can cause the head unwittingly to be thrust a few inches closer to the music. Having the head too far forward is a problem particularly for cellists, bassists, trombonists, and others who are more constrained by their instruments.

Posture, freedom, and ease of playing also play a role in neck disorders, and approaches such as the Alexander Technique and Feldenkrais "Awareness Through Movement" can be very helpful in treatment and prevention of injury. It's usually a good idea to have a medical diagnosis to rule out more serious disorders such as nerve compression (pinched nerve) from arthritis, or a herniated ("slipped") disk. Nerve pain often has an electrical or "pins and needles" quality and is more likely to radiate down the arm (radiculitis). While these conditions can and do occur in musicians, muscular problems are far more common.

There are non-instrumental causes of discomfort, also. One of the chief culprits that often goes unrecognized is the telephone. Those of us who unfortunately have to spend quite a bit of time on the phone must guard against holding the phone between the ear and the shoulder, as this can be a significant source of neck discomfort, promoting not only pain and muscle spasm, but shortening of the muscles on the side where the telephone is habitually held. At the least, I recommend getting a telephone shoulder rest. Even better options include holding the telephone with the hand, using a speaker phone, or obtaining a headset.

Another activity that needs to be discussed is sleeping and the use of certain pillows. Many of us sleep in rather awkward postures, which can contribute to neck pain. Orthopedically-designed pillows made of specially sculpted foam, such as the Wal-pillo or the egg-crate pillow, cradle the head and maintain the cervical spine in a neutral alignment during sleeping.

Another factor that can be overlooked is the positioning of music relative to the performer. I observed a pit drummer in a major show spend about fourteen measures playing his tom-tom on the far right side of his setup while craning his neck 180° to read the music on the left. Simply photocopying that one section of music and putting it above the tom-tom alleviated his neck strain. Similarly, sharing a stand and looking crosswise at the music while trying to watch the conductor can be a physical challenge!

Summary

Many problems in the neck region can be prevented by performing proper warm-up and conditioning exercises, paying attention to posture, and, on occasion, modifying the instrument or customizing chin or shoulder rests. Making music needn't be a pain in the neck!

Suggested Reading

Kamwendo K; Linton SJ. A controlled study of the effect of neck strain in medical secretaries. *Scandanavian Journal of Rehabilitation Medicine* 1991; 23(3): 143-52.

Lederman RJ. Peripheral nerve disorders in instrumentalists. *Annals of Neurology* 1989 Nov; 26(5): 640-46.

Linton SJ; Kamwendo K. Risk factors in the psychosocial work environment for neck and shoulder pain in secretaries. *Journal of Occupational Medicine* 1989 Jul; 31(7): 609-13.

Makela M; Heliovaara M; Sievers K; Impivaara O; Knekt P; Aromaa A. Prevalence, determinants, and consequences of chronic neck pain in Finland. *American Journal of Epidemiology* 1991 Dec 1; 134(11): 1356-67.

Newmark J; Rybock JD. Post-traumatic cervical disc herniation in a professional bass player: the importance of occupational pain. *Medical Problems of Performing Artists* 1990 Jun; 5(2): 89-90.

Chapter 4

Thoracic Outlet Syndrome

Thoracic outlet syndrome (TOS) represents a continuum of symptoms that frequently afflict musicians and are often difficult to diagnose. The main features include fatigue or numbness of the hand or arm with use, nonspecific aching of the limb(s), and vascular changes causing coldness or discoloration of the hands. Some other syndromes that could be mistaken for TOS include carpal tunnel syndrome, cubital tunnel syndrome (nerve compression at the elbow), pinched nerve in the neck, and Raynaud's disease (extreme coldness with color changes of the hands).

Anatomy

The thoracic outlet refers to the area of the body where the neck, chest, and shoulder meet and through which pass the major nerves and blood vessels on their way to the arm and hand. As they travel their course, the nerves and blood vessels are susceptible to compression in several locations (Fig. 1): between the muscles on the side of the neck (scalenes), especially if these muscles are tight or have an abnormal configuration (anatomic variation); between the collar bone (clavicle) and the first rib; and between the chest (pectoral) muscles and the ribs. Other anatomic variations such as a rudimentary rib coming off the last cervical (neck) vertebra can also cause or contribute to TOS. Low-slung, droopy shoulders can predispose to TOS, as can tight pectorals, often seen in cellists, woodwind players, pianists, and performers of other instruments in which the arms are held in front of the body or wrapped around the instrument for long periods of time. Also vulnerable are players who have a "collapsed chest" posture when they play. Most often affected are the left arms of string players (especially double bassists, guitarists, and harpists), and the right arms of flutists and horn players (depending on how these instruments are held). Of particular concern are heavy

29

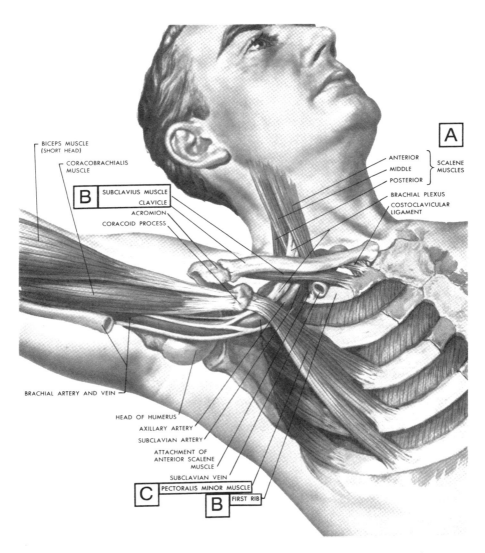

Figure 1: The three main sites of neurovascular compression: A) between the scalene neck muscles; B) between the clavicle (collarbone) and the first rib; and C) underneath the origin of the pectoralis minor muscle. As illustrated, the compression is increased with elevation of the arm, a frequent occurrence in the left arms of some string players playing in certain positions.

Reprinted by permission of CIBA *Clinical Symposia* 1973; 23(2).

instruments, such as guitar and accordion, supported with a strap, as the downward traction on the shoulder girdle can cause vascular compression or traction on the nerves. Carrying heavy bags, instruments, amplifiers, or suitcases can cause similar problems. Heavy backpacks should have waistbands to take stress off of the shoulders.

Diagnosis

In the great majority of cases, the symptoms are caused by compression or stretching of the nerves and, occasionally, the blood vessels, although electrodiagnostic testing, as was discussed for the diagnosis of carpal tunnel, is often negative. Vascular studies, such as angiograms and venograms (whereby dye is injected in order to show the blood vessels on x-ray), can be dangerous and are reserved for exceptional cases. In most cases, the diagnosis is a clinical one, based on physical examination and history.

The symptoms of TOS are often positional, especially when the arm is elevated or brought behind the body. This partially pinches off the blood supply or stretches the nerves, so that when the person undertakes muscular effort such as playing an instrument, the muscles lack adequate blood supply, and pain and coldness ensue.

In addition to observing the playing position, I often perform the elevated arm stress test (EAST) in the office: the patient is asked to hold both arms overhead, elbows and shoulders at 90°, and slowly open and close both hands for up to sixty seconds. If TOS is present, this test will usually trigger the symptoms. How rapidly the test provokes symptoms and how rapidly the symptoms disappear once the test is stopped can give some clinical indication of severity.

Treatment

The treatment of TOS depends on an accurate diagnosis. The application of heat (hot shower, hot packs, or heating pad, etc.)

to the neck and upper chest for ten to fifteen minutes should be followed by slow, sustained stretching exercises to the muscles on the side of the neck (ear towards shoulder—Fig. 2) and to the pectorals (Fig. 3). The pectorals can be stretched by facing towards a corner of the room with one hand on each wall at about shoulder height and gently leaning forward until the elbows are slightly behind the body. Each stretch should be held for about thirty seconds, released, and repeated two or three times. For reasons previously mentioned, the pectoral stretch is also a good preventive maneuver for cellists, woodwind players, and pianists.

Strengthening the muscles that support the shoulder girdle is necessary as well. These include the trapezius (the muscle between the neck and shoulder where shoulder straps rest) and the rhomboids (the muscles between the shoulder blades). The trapezius is strengthened by performing shoulder shrugs against resistance; the rhomboids, by leaning in towards the corner of a room with one's back to the corner, elbows bent at right angles and held against the rib cage. The forearms are then rotated outward, away from the body, until they contact the wall, and are then pressed firmly against the wall until the muscle contraction is felt (Fig. 4). Three or four contractions held for six seconds are sufficient. People with TOS are advised to do these exercises under the guidance of a physical therapist. The video "Therapeutic Exercise for Musicians" (see chapter 13) covers these and other exercises.

As posture often plays a significant role in TOS, movement re-education techniques such as Alexander and Feldenkrais can be very helpful, especially in conjunction with video feedback.

Surgery is only occasionally necessary and is reserved for severe symptoms not relieved by other forms of treatment.

Figure 2
neck stretches
for scalenes

Figure 3
pectoral stretches

Figure 4
strengthening the
interscapular
muscles
(rhomboids)

References

Roos, D. Thoracic Outlet Syndrome in Musicians. *Journal of Hand Therapy* 1992 May-June; 5(2): 65-72.

Chapter 5

Back Problems in Musicians: Causes and Types

Back problems in musicians have a variety of manifestations. Pain can occur in either the upper or lower back; can be acute or chronic; and can be primarily muscular, ligamentous, or neurogenic in origin. Let's look at each one of these in turn.

The most common type of back pain in musicians and in the general population is musculoskeletal strain from various causes. By comparison, back pain of neurologic origin (most commonly from either a herniated lumbar disk or from arthritic impingement of the nerves) is relatively uncommon. Diskogenic back pain usually radiates down the backs of the legs and may cause burning, numbness, or localized muscle weakness.

Sitting is the most uncomfortable position for people with most types of low back pain. Back pain may be either primarily related to playing an instrument or, as one of the most common human afflictions, may be from causes extraneous to playing the instrument but aggravated by musical activity. Both upper and lower back pain are common.

There are certain instruments that by their very nature predispose the instrumentalist to back problems. As was discussed in chapter 3, a poorly conditioned body is a setup for musculoskeletal problems. Muscles that are tight and weak are much more susceptible to strain and pain than are strong and flexible muscles.

Besides the upper and lower back muscles themselves, the key muscles involved in back problems are the hamstrings and the abdominal muscles. The hamstrings originate at the pelvis (sitting bones) and insert below the knee. When these muscles are tight, which is extremely common unless one undertakes a specific therapeutic stretching exercise program, they have the effect of tethering the pelvis; thus, when one bends forward, instead of normal forward pelvic rotation and flexion of the lumbar spine, all the flexion takes place in the spine alone, increasing the strain on the low back. Also, because the abdominal contents are primarily liquid, strong abdominal muscles have a sort of hydraulic effect of stiffening the whole region, thereby alleviating some of the load that the lumbar muscles must carry. In summary, a good therapeutic exercise program addresses strength and flexibility of the upper and lower back muscles and also includes hamstring stretching and abdominal strengthening.

Back Problems in Cellists

Back problems in cellists are often related to the sitting posture. Sitting with the knees and hips flexed at 90° is very stressful for the low back. In addition to a good therapeutic exercise program, the use of a forward-sloping seat will put the lumbar spine in a more natural position, thereby helping to alleviate low back strain. (More on this later.)

Good practice habits—limiting the playing sessions to perhaps forty or fifty minutes at a time and then taking a break to do some limbering-up exercises—can help to alleviate back strain. The harp and the cello tend to cause back strain primarily because there is limited opportunity to move around freely while one is playing.

The length of the cello end pin can be critical in back problems. Many cellists like to hunch forward around the instrument because it makes them feel more intimately involved with the cello and because they often feel psychologically exposed and uncomfortable when sitting up in a straight position. In order to sit up straight, one must lengthen the end pin to avoid having the tuning peg stuck in one's ears! The angled or "Rostropovich" end pin (invented by Tortelier) is often preferred because it enables gravity to assist the arms in playing by bringing the fingerboard into a more horizontal position, thus reducing the need for muscular effort. Angling the end pin brings more of the weight of the cello over the point of floor support, thereby decreasing the amount of weight borne by the chest and minimizing the backward thrust of torque that tends to "collapse" the chest and cause rounding or slumping of the back. This will be discussed in conjunction with seating posture. The combination of a forward-sloping seat and an angled end pin is probably the least stressful on the cellist's back. However, the angled end pin does pose some drawbacks for the bow arm (see chapter 6).

The cellist should tip the instrument slightly to the left side and keep the spine straight, rather than holding the instrument straight and inclining the spine to the right to accommodate the instrument. As gamba players use no end pin, the gamba tends to slip down little by little, until the instrumentalist winds up rather hunched over the instrument. We have been experimenting with using very small pads of thin material with a high coefficient of friction (dycem) between the calves and the instrument to prevent downward slippage.

Carrying and Lifting

Carrying instruments and accessories such as amplifiers is quite often a source of back problems. Proper body mechanics must be observed when lifting anything, not only musical instruments. One should bend from the knees instead of from the waist and should hold the weight as close to the body as possible. To be properly balanced, heavy instruments such as cellos, bassoons, and horns should have a long strap so that they can be placed over the head and hung across the body diagonally rather than hung from the shoulder on the same side. Even heavy music bags should be carried in this fashion to avoid undue strain. When carrying objects for long distances, switching them periodically from side to side will help to maintain balance. Gig bags that have padded, backpack-style straps in addition to a traditional grip can be ordered from

> Donna Altieri
> 5 South Fox St.
> Denver, CO 80223

I have also seen a very nice setup in which regular heavy-duty backpack straps and a waist strap were affixed to a cello case! Some cello cases now have built-in wheels—useful for long corridors in airport terminals!

Problems of Seating

When is a chair not a chair? When it is an instrument of torture! Musicians, along with students and other seated workers, are often unintentional victims of poorly designed seating. As Dr. A. C. Mandal points out in his book *The Seated Man*[1], the human body was not designed to sit with the hips and knees bent at a 90° angle. The chair as we know it seems to have been derived from the ancient throne—designed for ruling, not for working or for playing musical instruments! The chair as a symbol of power gives us the modern title "chairperson."

The International Conference of Symphony and Opera Musicians (ICSOM) conducted a survey in 1986 regarding the incidence of musculoskeletal problems in instrumentalists.[2] The survey revealed a high incidence of lower and upper back pain. Another study, reported in the *New York Times* science section (October 17, 1989), indicated a very high incidence of back pain in instrumentalists.

Back pain in the sitting position has several causes: poorly designed chairs, poorly conditioned backs, inadequate body awareness, and physical/emotional tension. Having a properly designed chair is no more a substitute for proper physical conditioning and body awareness than is taking vitamin pills a substitute for eating properly! There are now many physical therapists, Alexander teachers, and Feldenkrais practitioners who are skilled in working with performing artists and who can be a good resource for exercises and body awareness. Before beginning an exercise program, it is prudent to consult a physician to rule out medical causes of back pain.

The Mechanics of Sitting

When the hips are flexed at 90° (Fig. 1), the femur (thigh bone) can rotate only 60° in the hip socket. The remaining 30° comes from a posterior (backward) rotation of the pelvis[3]. Because the spine is attached to the pelvis, backward rotation of the pelvis causes flattening of the lumbar curve (lordosis), thereby placing the center of gravity of the torso approximately three inches behind the "sitting bones," creating a torque or turning force on the back.[4] This flattening of the lumbar curve and posterior pelvic tilt results in a slumped "C" curve to the entire spine (Fig. 2). To resist these forces in order to sit up straight, the abdominal, back extensor, and hip flexor muscles have to contract continuously. Continuous contraction of a muscle reduces its blood flow, resulting in the buildup of metabolites (waste products of muscle work). When metabolites accumulate, they cause pain, resulting in muscle spasm, and a vicious cycle of more pain and spasm ensues.[5] Flattening of the lumbar curve has other painful consequences, such as putting increased pressure on the intervertebral disks[6,7] and stretching the capsules of the small facet joints (the places where each vertebra contacts the next one above and below).[8]

For woodwind players, a further consideration is diaphragm function. The diaphragm is a large, dome-shaped muscle arising from the lower aspect of the ribs and sternum (breast bone) and inserting on the upper lumbar vertebrae. Flattening of the lumbar spine results in flattening of the diaphragm, limiting its excursion and thereby decreasing the air flow (Fig. 4).

The use of a forward-sloping seat can alleviate many problems, such as diminished breathing capacity and strain on the back muscles and ligaments, arising from the flattening of the lumbar curve. With the hips at 90°, the center of gravity is three inches behind the sitting bones, with the lumbar curve flattened 30°. If the seat is sloped forward 30°, the torso is brought directly over the sitting bones, eliminating the torque that would otherwise force the back into a "C" curve.[9] One can then maintain an erect posture with little muscular effort. This naturally occurs while standing (Fig. 3) and while sitting on a horse with one's thighs sloping downward. No backrest is needed! A full 30° slope is neither necessary nor desirable, for many people will feel pitched forward; a 15° or 20° slope seems to be adequate.

The principle of sloping forward while sitting can be seen in historical illustrations of seated workers from ancient Egypt to nineteenth-century Europe, but seems to have been forgotten by the designers of "modern" chairs until the recent advent of Scandinavian kneeling chairs, which have gained some popularity among seated workers. The chief disadvantages of the kneeling chairs are knee discomfort, as weight is loaded on the knees in an acutely flexed position (Fig. 3d); lack of portability (critical to musicians); and expense (even more critical to musicians)! A more practical solution for musicians who travel and therefore are subjected to sitting on house chairs (often standard folding chairs), or for anyone who spends the working day in a chair, is a lightweight, portable wedge cushion to modify the existing chair seat. The ErgoCush, catalog #1177, is available from

AliMed® Inc.
297 High St.
Dedham, MA 02026
(800) 225-2610

This cushion allows the back to assume a comfortable position similar to that obtained by using a kneeling chair, but without the accompanying knee discomfort. A dual-layer foam system provides both comfort and firm support, and a black velveteen cover prevents down-sliding.

Even less expensive are other alternatives, such as placing a rolled towel at the rear of the seat or placing a two-by-four-inch board under the back legs of the chair. (While observing a recent youth symphony orchestra rehearsal, I noted that several wind and string players tipped their backward-sloping chairs onto the front legs to attain a forward-sloping effect!)

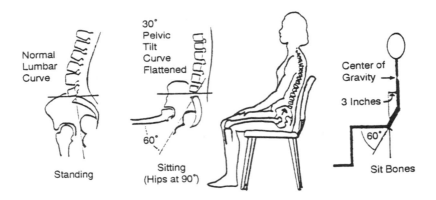

Figure 1
In sitting with the hips flexed at 90°, the femur can rotate only 60° in the hip socket, so the pelvis must tilt backwards the other 30°, causing reversal of the normal lumbar curve.

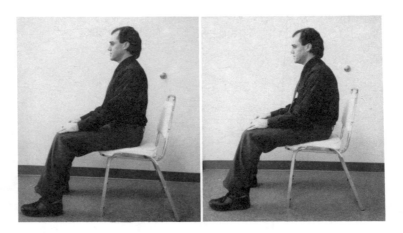

Figure 2
Since the center of gravity is now behind the sitting bones, considerable muscular force is needed to sit upright (left). Relaxing (giving in to the force) results in a slumped "C" curve of the spine (right).

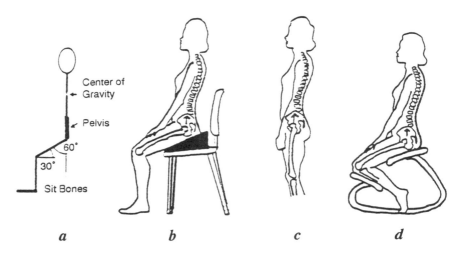

Figure 3
The forward-sloping seat places the center of gravity directly over the sitting bones (Figs. 3a, 3b). This is similar to the standing position (Fig. 3c). The kneeling chair (Fig. 3d) loads weight on the knees in an acutely flexed position.

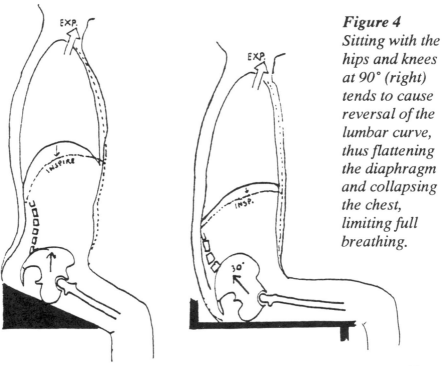

Figure 4
Sitting with the hips and knees at 90° (right) tends to cause reversal of the lumbar curve, thus flattening the diaphragm and collapsing the chest, limiting full breathing.

42

Summary

Seat modification is only a battle in the war against back discomfort. Through a good exercise program of strength and flexibility, frequent breaks to change position during practice, attention to body awareness by such means as yoga, Alexander, or Feldenkrais work, and relaxation techniques such as meditation, biofeedback, or stress management programs, the musician can be free of the physical discomfort that so often takes the joy out of playing.

References

1. Mandal, A.C. *The Seated Man.* Copenhagen: Dafnia Press, 1985.

2. Middlestadt, SE. and Fishbein, M. The prevalence of severe musculoskeletal problems among male and female symphony orchestra string players. *Medical Problems of Performing Artists* 1989 March; 4(1): 44.

3. Schoberth, H. *Sitzhaltung, Sitzschaden, Sitmobel.* Berlin-Gottigen-Heidelberg: Springer-Verlag, 1962.

4. Mandal. *op. cit.*, 33.

5. Cailliet, R. *Low Back Pain Syndrome.* Philadelphia: F.A. Davis, 1983, 214.

6. Nachemson, A. The load on lumbar disks in different positions of the body. *Clinical Orthopedics* 1966; 45: 107-22.

7. Nachemson, A. Intervertebral dynamic pressure measurement in lumbar disks. *Scandinavian Journal of Rehabilitation Medicine* 1970: supplement 1.

8. Keegan, J.J. *Journal of Bone and Joint Surgery* 1953 July; 35A:(3).

9. Mandal, A.C. *op. cit.*, 33.

Orchestra Chairs by David DeGroot *(facing page)*

Reprinted by permission of *Senza Sordino* (April 1990) and David DeGroot.

OBOE CHAIR

FRENCH HORN CHAIR

TROMBONE CHAIR

VIOLIN CHAIR

VIOLA CHAIR

CELLO CHAIR

PERCUSSION CHAIR

CONDUCTOR CHAIR

HARP CHAIR

Chapter 6

Shoulder Problems

The shoulder, which is the most mobile joint in the body, allows the hand to be positioned over a wide range. Such mobility is not without its price, however, as the shoulder is also the least stable joint. The shoulder actually is a very sophisticated complex of joints, including the shoulder joint proper (glenohumeral), the collar bone (clavicle), and the articulation of the shoulder blade (scapula) with the rib cage (thorax).

There are two principal muscle groups acting on the shoulder joint. The large superficial muscle that gives the shoulder its contour is called the deltoid. Its chief functions are to move the arm away from the body (abduction) and to draw the arm forward (flexion) or backward (extension). Deep in the deltoid is the rotator cuff—a group of four muscles originating from both sides of the scapula and blending together, forming a cuff as they insert on the rounded, upper end of the arm bone (humeral head) at the shoulder joint. The chief function of the rotator cuff muscles is to stabilize the head of the humerus in the shallow joint socket as the deltoid moves the arm. The cuff also rotates the shoulder. Between the cuff and the deltoid muscle are the bony arch of the shoulder and a collapsed sac (bursa) that facilitates smooth shoulder motion (Fig. 1).

When the arm is rotated in towards the body and then brought away from the body (abducted), the rotator cuff and bursa get pinched between a bony prominence on the head of the humerus and the overlying bony arch (Fig. 2). This can lead to tendinitis, bursitis, and disabling pain.

Cellists are often affected in the shoulder of the right arm, especially when bowing on the A-string. One remedy that has been suggested to me by a cellist is to sit with the back rotated around to the right, thereby decreasing the amount of internal rotation needed at the shoulder to bow to the tip on the A-string.

While this may work, I would be concerned about the asymmetry of the posture and the strain imposed on the back muscles. Another solution is to rotate the cello slightly in towards the bow arm when playing on the A-string. Of course, the cello must then be rotated back when playing on the C-string. The freedom of motion required to accomplish this rotation is probably easier to attain with a straight end pin than with an angled end pin, because the instrument is pivoting about its axis. In addition, the use of an angled end pin usually requires the right arm to be held higher (abducted), due to the increased angle of the fingerboard. A higher right arm might allow for less muscular effort by taking advantage of the force of gravity acting on the bow arm, but might also increase the risk of shoulder impingement.

For the "chin strings," the right side of the instrument may be lowered so as to decrease the amount of abduction/internal rotation occuring at the right shoulder when bowing on the lower strings. Again, this has to be weighed against possible difficulties in bowing on the higher strings. In Yehudi Menuhin's *Music Guides* on violin and viola, William Primrose advocates keeping the right elbow down. A lower right elbow will decrease the risk of bursitis/tendinitis from impingement.

In classical guitarists, right shoulder problems are also common, but for different reasons. The player usually thrusts the right shoulder forward, so as to be able to lay the forearm flat against the guitar and avoid impinging the underside of the right forearm against the sharp edge of the guitar. This position strains the shoulder muscles and tendons. There is no easy answer, as the problem really lies with instrument design. Electric guitarists with a thinner instrument do not have this problem.

The most important part of treating shoulder tendinitis or bursitis consists of avoiding pain-producing activities, especially overhead or reaching-behind movements. Also helpful are massage, anti-inflammatory medications such as aspirin or ibuprofen, and the application of ice packs.

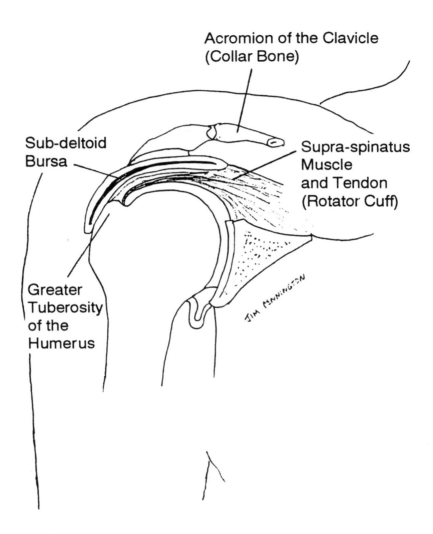

Acromion of the Clavicle
(Collar Bone)

Sub-deltoid
Bursa

Supra-spinatus
Muscle
and Tendon
(Rotator Cuff)

Greater
Tuberosity
of the
Humerus

Figure 1
Right shoulder seen from the front

Site of Impingement

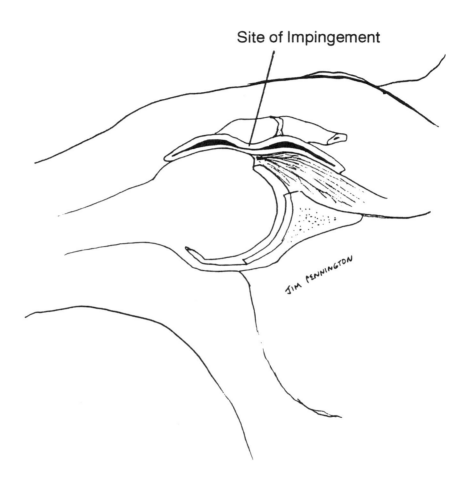

Figure 2
Right shoulder seen from the front
When the arm is abducted past 90°, the greater tuberosity of
the humerus compresses the rotator cuff against the acromion,
causing pain and decreased motion in the shoulder.

Therapeutic exercises to increase the strength and endurance of the cuff muscles might also offer some protection against overuse and impingement. Appropriate exercises would consist of gentle but progressive resistance to rotational shoulder movements using either a light dumbbell or elastic band (Thera-band). Further details about therapeutic exercise can be obtained from the video mentioned in chapter 13 or by consulting a physical therapist.

The rotator cuff tendons have rather poor blood supply in their central portion. Persons having to carry instruments, amplifiers, or other heavy loads for long distances should be aware that the blood supply of these tendons is further compromised by traction, such as when hanging heavy loads from the end of the arm. The use of a broad shoulder strap slung over the head and worn across the chest can save wear-and-tear on the rotator cuff. When using backpacks to carry books, both straps should be worn to avoid stressing one shoulder. Backpack-style gig bags are available for brass, woodwinds, or strings from

> Donna Altieri
> 5 South Fox St.
> Denver, CO 80223

The rotator cuff can be injured in nonmusical activities as well. Working for prolonged periods with the arms overhead, such as when house-painting, can stress the shoulder area. Frequent rest periods are helpful. I have treated several cuff injuries sustained from the Nautilus chest-exercise machine and from playing tug-of-war with the Labrador retriever!

Finally, it should be carefully noted that a variety of medical illnesses, ranging from gall bladder disease and lung tumors to slipped cervical disks, can cause referred pain in the shoulder. Merely treating symptoms without a specific medical diagnosis is imprudent.

Chapter 7

The Cubital Tunnel Syndrome: Nerve Entrapment at the Elbow

Nerve entrapment at the elbow is common among musicians. Unlike tendinitis or muscle strain, irritated nerve tissue does not respond quickly to physical therapy or medications. Rest and early recognition of the syndrome are of the utmost importance in preventing more severe nerve damage and its consequences, such as muscle wasting (atrophy).

Nerve entrapment at the elbow is characterized by pain, particularly on the inner or medial side. This pain often radiates down the pinkie (ulnar) side of the forearm and into the pinkie side of the hand. There may also be other signs of nerve irritation such as numbness, "pins and needles" sensations, and, in the worst scenario, muscle wasting. Symptoms are often aggravated when the elbow is bent (flexed) as opposed to when the arm is held out straight (extended).

The anatomy of the ulnar region interacts with certain instruments to predispose those instrumentalists to cubital tunnel syndrome. The cubital tunnel is located on the inner aspect of the elbow (Fig. 1), in the area where the nerve to the pinkie side of the elbow (the ulnar nerve) runs in the groove on the "funny bone." In this region, the ulnar nerve is susceptible to trauma from external pressure or compression, which can be one cause of cubital tunnel syndrome, though not the usual cause in musicians. The floor of the tunnel is made up of the joint capsule and the muscles that flex the fingers (flexor digitorum profundus). The sides of the tunnel are made up of the two heads of the flexor carpi ulnaris muscle, which flexes the wrist (brings the palm towards the forearm) and also deviates it towards the pinkie side (ulnar deviation). The roof of the tunnel is formed by a dense, unyielding ligament.

When the elbow is flexed, the tunnel is passively narrowed and the ulnar nerve is stretched in its groove. Positions of extreme elbow flexion are seen in the left arms of cellists and bassists playing in first position, and in the right arms of piccolo players.

Violinists have a somewhat different problem with this syndrome than cellists do. Although the elbow never is as flexed playing the violin as it is playing the cello, the left arm is twisted (supinated), which puts an additional strain on the nerve. The flexor carpi ulnaris muscles, which form the sides of the tunnel and surround the ulnar nerve, are the very muscles that are used in playing in seventh position and above on the violin, and contraction of these muscles contributes to additional nerve compression.

Possibly, people who develop cubital tunnel syndrome have a somewhat narrower tunnel. Playing with excessive tension in the left hand is another probable culprit. When playing *forte,* many string players have a tendency to increase the pressure of the left hand unnecessarily. Over time, this can lead to problems such as cubital tunnel syndrome and tendinitis.

Although cubital tunnel syndrome can be diagnosed clinically, definitive diagnosis is made by two types of electrodiagnostic testing: nerve conduction velocity studies (NCV) and electromyography (EMG). Nerve conduction velocity tests the speed at which the nerve conducts an electrical impulse. When a nerve is entrapped, irritated, or partially damaged, the nerve impulses are slowed across the damaged segment. Thus, by stimulating the nerve and measuring the velocity in different areas, one can ascertain where the nerve is being entrapped. The EMG consists of probing the muscles to look for electrical patterns characteristic of nerve damage. Indication of muscle damage is a more serious finding than damage to the sensory portion of the nerve. Findings of muscle damage may warrant earlier and more aggressive treatment.

Clinical findings include pain in the inner aspect of the elbow, and numbness and tingling in the pinkie side of the hand. These symptoms are provoked or worsened by sustained elbow flexion, which often causes sleep disturbances at night. In severe or chronic cases, signs of muscle atrophy can be seen in the muscle between the thumb and index finger (first dorsal interosseous muscle) and the muscles between the bones on the back of the hand (the dorsal interossei muscles). These muscles are innervated by the ulnar nerve (Fig. 1) and suffer when the nerve is damaged.

Figure 1 (facing page)
The ulnar nerve can be seen (in phantom) passing behind the medial epicondyle. Bending the elbow (flexion) stretches the nerve here. The nerve can also be entrapped at the wrist where it passes through its own tunnel (Guyon's canal). The ulnar nerve provides sensory (skin) input to the pinkie side of the hand and motor input to the small, intrinsic hand muscles that are very important for fine coordination.

Reprinted by permission, CIBA *Clinical Symposia* 1973; 23(2).

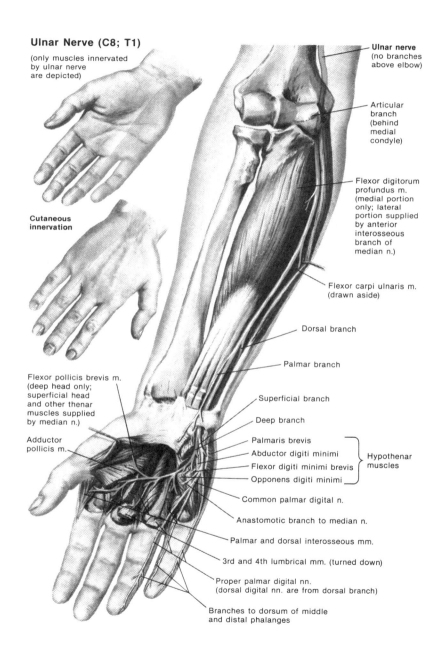

Ulnar Nerve (C8; T1)

(only muscles innervated by ulnar nerve are depicted)

Cutaneous innervation

Flexor pollicis brevis m. (deep head only; superficial head and other thenar muscles supplied by median n.)

Adductor pollicis m.

Ulnar nerve (no branches above elbow)

Articular branch (behind medial condyle)

Flexor digitorum profundus m. (medial portion only; lateral portion supplied by anterior interosseous branch of median n.)

Flexor carpi ulnaris m. (drawn aside)

Dorsal branch

Palmar branch

Superficial branch

Deep branch

Palmaris brevis
Abductor digiti minimi
Flexor digiti minimi brevis
Opponens digiti minimi

} Hypothenar muscles

Common palmar digital n.

Anastomotic branch to median n.

Palmar and dorsal interosseous mm.

3rd and 4th lumbrical mm. (turned down)

Proper palmar digital nn. (dorsal digital nn. are from dorsal branch)

Branches to dorsum of middle and distal phalanges

54

Treatment for cubital tunnel syndrome first of all depends on early recognition, when the problem is much easier to cure. Avoiding the position of extreme flexion of the elbow is very important and may require the use of a night splint to prevent sleeping with the elbow flexed. The splint should be made by an occupational therapist and should consist of a thermoplastic upper-arm band and a forearm band, joined by an adjustable hinge such as the Phoenix hinge made by Aquaplast (Fig. 2). The hinge should be set to allow the elbow to straighten completely, but to bend only about 35°. The forearm cuff should be lined with Tempra Foam for comfort. The splint should be worn as many hours per day as possible, and especially at night, when the elbow tends to be fully flexed for hours at a time. It may take a while to work up to full-time wear. An elbow pad, such as skateboarders wear, should be added to avoid direct compression to the nerve when leaning on the elbows (a position which one should try to minimize).

It may be necessary to wear the splint for ten to twelve weeks, or until the tingling and numbness subside. As the symptoms lessen, the hinge is adjusted to allow more and more elbow flexion. When over 100° of flexion is attained without provoking symptoms, the splint may be gradually discontinued (but not thrown away!) and normal activities resumed. Cellists should begin practicing in thumb position and gradually work towards first position. The "chin strings" would do the reverse, starting in first to third positions and gradually working up the neck. Piccolo players would practice on the flute.

It is probably best to avoid playing for at least a week or two to give the nerve a chance to recover. The musician who must continue either to practice or perform must minimize excessive left-hand tension and, if possible, avoid the aggravating positions. For example, a violinist could more safely play in the first and second positions and avoid playing in the higher positions.

Ultrasound such as is commonly used to treat muscle pain (1.5 to 2.0 watts/cm^2) can actually slow the healing of the nerve

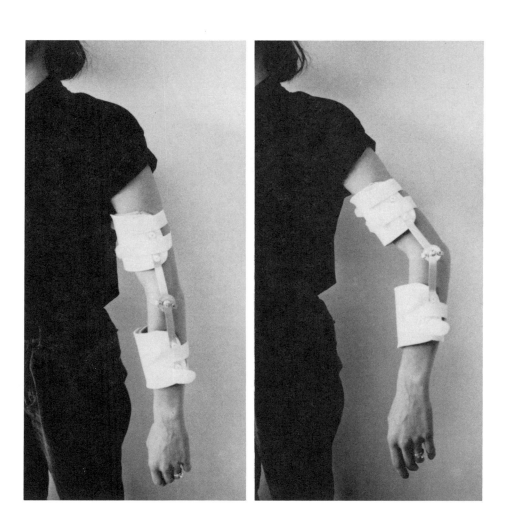

Figure 2
Hinged elbow splint allows full extension, but blocks full flexion.

and is not recommended. Cold packs are helpful (applied for ten minutes, two to three times per day), but ice may be too extreme and irritating. Oral anti-inflammatory medications are helpful; salicylate-based creams such as Aspercreme contain anti-inflammatory medication that can penetrate through the skin into the affected area. The treatment program of relative or complete rest, night or day splinting as necessary, cold packs, and anti-inflammatory medication should continue until the nerve is no longer tender to palpation in the groove on the inner aspect of the elbow, and until all other symptoms such as numbness and tingling (especially upon elbow flexion) have cleared up. Gentle strengthening exercises may be helpful if the arm has become somewhat weakened from disuse, but of greater importance is gradual return to playing (see chapter 14).

On occasion, the symptoms are so severe, particularly if there is evidence of muscle wasting, that a surgical release must be performed. There are several types of surgical procedures and quite a bit of controversy over which is best. Transpositions (moving the nerve to the front of the arm) are more technically demanding and tend to carry a higher risk, but can be effective if the surgeon is skillful. However, if cubital tunnel syndrome is recognized and treated early enough, it often resolves fairly quickly and well without surgery.

Suggested Reading

Charness ME; Barbaro NM; Olney RK; Parry GJ. Occupational cubital tunnel syndrome in instrumental musicians. *Neurology* 1987 Mar; 37(3 suppl 1): 115.

Charness ME; Parry GJ; Markison RE; Rosegay H; Barbaro NM. Entrapment neuropathies in musicians. *Neurology* 1985 Apr; 35(4 suppl 1): 74.

Dawson WJ. Reed-maker's elbow. *Medical Problems of Performing Artists* 1986 Mar; 1(1): 24.

Hotchkiss RN. Common disorders of the elbow in athletes and musicians. *Hand Clinics* 1990 Aug; 6(3): 507-15.

Maffulli N; Maffulli F. Transient entrapment neuropathy of the posterior interosseous nerve in violin players. *Journal of Neurology Neurosurgery and Psychiatry* 1991 Jan; 54(1): 65-67.

Chapter 8

Carpal Tunnel Syndrome

Carpal tunnel syndrome (CTS) is often in the news these days. Special focus is given to video display terminal (VDT) operators, but musicians and many other people who perform repetitive manual tasks are at risk for developing this common, yet often misunderstood, syndrome. Musicians need to know how CTS is diagnosed and identified and how it can be prevented and treated.

Anatomy

CTS refers to the symptoms of median nerve compression. The median nerve is a mixed nerve, so-called because it carries motor impulses to muscle and sensory impulses from skin. In the hand, the median nerve innervates the muscles at the base of the thumb (thenar muscles) and some of the muscles about the index and middle fingers (interosseous muscles). The median nerve runs along the underside of the forearm and enters the hand at the wrist through the carpal tunnel (Fig. 1), a space formed by the wrist (carpal) bones on the bottom and the dense, unyielding transverse carpal ligament across the top. The median nerve shares this space with the flexor tendons, which go to the thumb and fingers and control gripping. The median nerve lies between the tendons and the ligament and is very susceptible to compression between these structures.

Symptoms

The primary symptoms of CTS are pain, numbness, tingling, and, in more severe cases, muscle wasting (atrophy). These symptoms are usually localized to the thumb, index finger, middle finger, and half of the ring finger. In less severe cases, the symptoms are mild and occasional, often occurring in the morning or during the night. Over time, the symptoms may become more severe and constant. Sufferers often complain of clumsi-

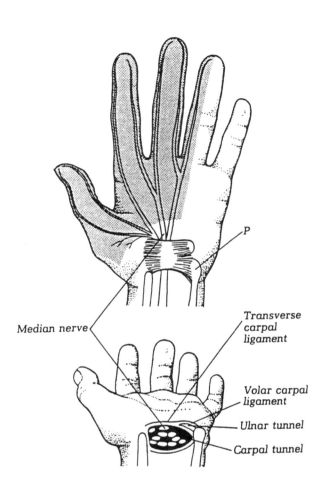

P

Median nerve

Transverse
carpal
ligament

Volar carpal
ligament

Ulnar tunnel

Carpal tunnel

Figure 1
Carpal tunnel syndrome (median nerve compression)

Reprinted from *The Hand: Examination and Diagnosis*, 2d ed., 1983. By permission of
the American Society for Surgery of the Hand.

ness, noting loss of dexterity and difficulty in manipulating small objects. Obviously, due to the great demands of their profession, loss of dexterity would become noticeable much earlier in instrumentalists than in the general population.

Causes

Repetitive hand motions can cause inflammation of the flexor tendons. The subsequent swelling of the tendons can then cause the median nerve to be compressed against the overlying ligament. Some people are born with a small carpal tunnel, making them more prone to develop problems. The fluid retention that accompanies pregnancy can also increase the pressure within the tunnel, causing nerve compression. This is usually self-limiting, clearing up without treatment after delivery.

Perhaps the most common cause in musicians is sustained or repetitive wrist flexion. A study done in 1981 by Gelberman showed that the pressure in the carpal tunnel increased dramatically as the wrist approached 90° of flexion or 90° of extension. Repetitive flexion and extension also resulted in a sustained elevation in pressure within the carpal tunnel. These extremes in wrist position are often seen in people playing in the higher positions on the violin. The viola, with its wider body, tends to cause an even greater degree of wrist flexion in high positions. Some string players allow the right wrist to flex excessively on the up-bow as the frog approaches the bridge. Placing a synthesizer on a surface that is too high can result in excessive wrist flexion. A distorted right-wrist position is often seen in bass guitarists who hold the instrument too high. A hyperextended left wrist is commonly seen in flutists, particularly when they attempt to hold the instrument very horizontally and with an in-line G-key. The list could go on and on. The key factor here is repetitive or sustained extremes of wrist position. To minimize carpal tunnel pressure, one should strive for a neutral wrist position when playing. If that is not possible, then one should practice in very brief segments those passages that require extreme flexion, interspersing them with practice of less stressful passages. Full pronation (palms down) has been shown by magnetic resonance imaging (MRI) to cause shifting of the flexor tendons against the median nerve. This poses a risk for pianists.

Diagnosis

The diagnosis of CTS is primarily by physical examination, although tests such as nerve conduction velocity studies can be useful for confirmation and clarification. Tingling and/or decreased sensation in the median nerve distribution (the thumb, index, middle, and half of the ring finger) is a typical finding. There is often pain or a feeling of electric shock running into the hand or up the arm when the median nerve is tapped at the wrist—the so-called Tinel's sign (Fig. 2). Holding the wrist in a fully flexed position for a minute or so will often provoke pain or numbness in the median nerve distribution—Phalen's sign. An indicator of the severity of the condition is how quickly the symptoms are provoked in testing for Phalen's sign and how long they take to disappear once the wrist flexion is released. Obvious signs of wasting or weakness of the thumb muscles indicate severe or long-standing disease and the need for a surgical consultation.

Figure 2
Tinel's sign

Reprinted from *The Hand: Examination and Diagnosis*, 2d ed., 1983. By permission of the American Society for Surgery of the Hand.

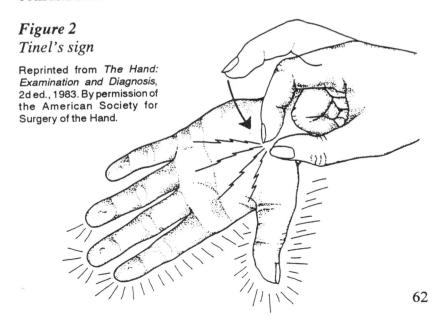

Electrodiagnostic testing can be useful in confirming the diagnosis, especially if surgery is recommended or contemplated. Testing is also useful because the median nerve can be compressed in locations other than the wrist, such as the forearm or the neck, producing a clinical picture very similar to CTS. Compression can also occur at multiple sites—the "double-crush" syndrome. In flutists and mallet players, the nerves that run alongside the fingers can be compressed, again causing symptoms similar to CTS.

Electrodiagnostic testing consists of electromyography (EMG) and nerve conduction velocity (NCV) tests. In the EMG, a fine, teflon-covered probe, similar to an acupuncture needle, is inserted into a muscle and the electrical activity is observed on a screen. Compression or damage to the nerve that stimulates that muscle produces a typical pattern of electrical activity. In the NCV, the nerve is electrically stimulated at a certain point. A surface electrode placed on the skin over the nerve at a different location registers the length of time the impulse takes to travel between the two points. Knowing the distance between the points allows one to calculate the velocity of the impulse. Nerve transmission is slowed across a compressed or damaged segment. About five to ten per cent of people with CTS will have a normal EMG/NCV, so the test results must always be correlated with the clinical picture. Conversely, many asymptomatic people have borderline slowing of the NCV across the wrist, and this should not be considered pathological. "Treat the patient, not the test results."

Treatment

A mainstay in the treatment of CTS is the use of wrist splints (Fig. 3). These devices leave the fingers free but stabilize the wrist, preventing flexion or extension. They can be purchased without prescription at most large pharmacies. For mild cases, one would begin by using them mostly at night, as many people sleep with their fists curled up and wrists flexed. If the symptoms do not subside within a week or two, the splints should be used during the day as well. Care should be taken to remove them every hour or two for five to ten minutes of gentle exercise to prevent wrist stiffness. The splints may be removed for instrumental practice, assuming that the practice does not provoke the rapid or severe onset of symptoms. Positions of increased wrist flexion must be avoided during practice. Sometimes splinting is only partially successful—although it keeps the wrist neutral, the CTS splint still allows grasping and opening of the fingers; thus, the flexor tendons are still rubbing against the inflamed median nerve. A full-length splint that immobilizes the fingers will prevent this. As always, the splint should be removed periodically for pain-free, range-of-motion exercises.

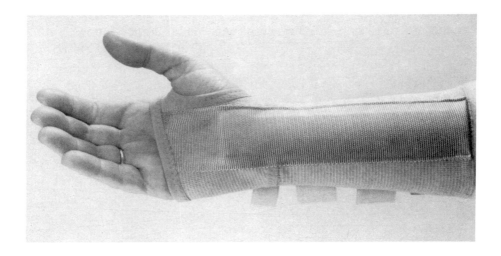

Figure 3
Carpal tunnel splint; note the stiff bar that immobilizes the wrist.

Photo courtesy of AliMed; reprinted by permission.

In addition to splinting, other modalities that are often helpful are the moderate use (five minutes) of ice massage to reduce inflammation, low-dose ultrasound treatments, and anti-inflammatory medications (aspirin, ibuprofen, Naprosyn, etc.). To prevent stomach irritation, these medicines must be taken with food. There is no evidence, to my knowledge, that joint manipulation at the wrist or the neck is therapeutic for CTS. Diet is important, but has not been shown to affect the course of CTS, with the possible exception of vitamin B$_6$ supplements at a recommended dosage of 200 milligrams per day.

I am not a surgeon and certainly do not rush to send my patients to surgery. However, if there is evidence of muscle wasting; if the pain, numbness, or tingling are so severe and persistent that they become disabling to one's musical career or daily activities; or if the nonsurgical treatment outlined above does not clear the symptoms in six weeks or so, then a surgical consultation is warranted. Surgery for CTS has a fairly high success rate for relieving symptoms. While complications are always a possibility with any operation, they are relatively uncommon in this procedure. The most common reasons for unsuccessful surgery are failure to diagnose additional sites of nerve compression ("double-crush"), or failure to explore thoroughly and decompress the median nerve at the wrist.

Summary

Carpal tunnel syndrome is a common condition afflicting musicians and non-musicians alike. The principal, preventable cause is sustained or repetitive wrist flexion or extension, usually occupationally induced. By paying careful attention to instrumental technique, especially wrist position, and limiting the time spent in the extremes of flexion or extension, one can minimize the chance of developing this often disabling condition. Early recognition and treatment can nip the problem in the bud.

Suggested Reading

Dawson DM; Hallet M; Millender LH. *Entrapment Neuropathies.* 2d ed. Boston: Little Brown, 1990, chap. 19.

Eaton RG; Nolan WB. Diagnosis and surgical treatment of the hand. In: Sataloff RT; Brandfonbrener AG; Lederman RJ. *Textbook of Performing Arts Medicine.* New York: Raven Press, 1990, 205-28.

Fry HJH. Overuse syndrome in musicians—100 years ago. An historical review. *Medical Journal of Australia* 1986 Dec 1-15; 145(11-12): 620-25.

Lederman RJ. Nerve entrapment syndromes in instrumental musicians. *Medical Problems of Performing Artists* 1986 Jun; 1(2): 45-48.

Sternbach DJ. Carpal tunnel syndrome: what to know about it, what to do about it. *International Musician* 1991 Jul; 90(1): 8-9, 11.

Chapter 9

De Quervain's Disease:
Tendinitis at the Base of the Thumb

Anatomy

Tendinitis at the base of the thumb is so specific an entity that it even has its own name: de Quervain's disease. Prompt identification of this painful condition is important, because the tendons can develop thin wisps of scar tissue (adhesions), leading to chronic problems.

The two involved tendons are the abductor pollicus longus (APL) and the extensor pollicus brevis (EPB), part of a group called extensor tendons, which are located on the back of the wrist (Fig. 1). The APL and EPB are found within the first of a group of six compartments formed by dense bands of connective tissue. A unique aspect of the tendons of the first compartment is that they must pass through a rather tight, fibro-osseous tunnel (first dorsal extensor compartment) at the thumb side of the wrist, making them particularly susceptible to irritation or inflammation (tendinitis). Another vulnerability is that one of the forearm bones (the radius) flares out near the base of the thumb just where the first tunnel is located, creating mechanical stress on the tendons.

Anatomical variations can play a role as well. Multiple compartments or accessory (extra) tendons are often present, increasing the volume, and thus the friction, within the canal. Anatomical variation is very important for the surgeon to keep in mind, as one common cause of surgical failure is inadequate decompression or release of the entrapped tendons.

Positional Factors

The tendons become aggravated by certain characteristic movements, especially ulnar deviation (turning the hand and wrist toward the pinkie side). Strain on the tendons increases

67

when the thumb is brought under the hand towards the pinkie, as in holding the bow or in playing arpeggios on the piano. There is additional strain while playing up-bow, when the wrist is sometimes brought into a position of extreme ulnar deviation. When the hand and wrist are in a position of pronation/ulnar deviation/thumb adduction, the skin nerve in this region (superficial branch of the radial nerve) is also prone to injury or irritation. String players should be careful to avoid a position of extreme ulnar deviation in the wrist when playing up-bow at the frog. The acute flexion of the left wrist occurring during big stretches or in the highest positions on the "chin strings" also causes the tendons to pull around a sharp angle, with a resulting increase in friction. Ulnar deviation is common in percussionists, the left hands of trumpeters (depending on which finger is placed through the ring), the right hands of electric-bass guitarists, and the right hands of harpists in the high positions unless the right elbow is held up (abducted) as in the Salzedo technique. Not all instrumentalists will develop this problem, but there are certain occupational hazards.

The "New Arrival"

De Quervain's occurs in the general population as well. One of the factors, believe it or not, is the arrival of a new baby in the family! It's not uncommon for adults to develop this tendinitis from frequently lifting the baby by grasping with the two thumbs pointing up. The baby's weight forces the hands down into ulnar deviation, stressing the first compartment tendons as they resist the downward force. The supported weight quickly gets heavier as the baby grows!

Differential Diagnosis

There are two similar entities that are often confused with de Quervain's, but can usually be distinguished by physical exam. These are (1) osteoarthritis and (2) entrapment of the superficial branch of the radial nerve.

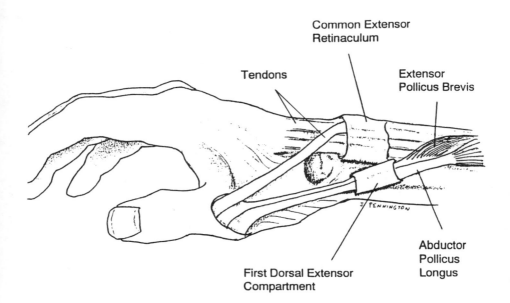

Common Extensor
Retinaculum

Tendons

Extensor
Pollicus Brevis

Abductor
Pollicus
Longus

First Dorsal Extensor
Compartment

Figure 1
Anatomy of the first dorsal extensor compartment

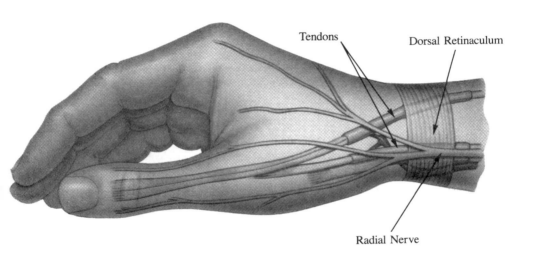

Figure 2
Note the superficial branch of the radial nerve overlying the
first dorsal extensor compartment.

Reprinted with permission from *Resident & Staff Physician* © June 1982 by Romaine Pierson Publishers, Inc.

Osteoarthritis at the base of the thumb (the carpometacarpal joint) is quite common in the general population, and the carpo-metacarpal joint is often one of the first joints to be affected. In osteoarthritis, pain will occur in the same location as in de Quervain's disease, but can usually be differentiated by gently compressing the long bone of the thumb (metacarpal) in towards the wrist bones and gently rotating it back and forth while maintaining the compression. This maneuver (the "grind" test) does not usually cause pain with tendinitis, but will cause discom-fort with arthritis. The Finklestein test consists of wrapping the fingers around the thumb, which is first tucked into the palm, and then causing ulnar deviation by bending the fist toward the pinkie (Fig. 3). Pain with this maneuver constitutes a positive response, indicating either de Quervain's disease or entrapment of the radial nerve; the response is usually negative with arthritis.

Entrapment of the superficial branch of the radial nerve (SBR), previously mentioned, does have a positive Finklestein test. This nerve provides feeling to the back of the thumb and back of the hand below the index and middle fingers and lies directly over the de Quervain tendons (Fig. 1). When the nerve is irritated, the stretch resulting from the ulnar deviation of the Finklestein test will be painful. However, the pain is often felt as burning, electric, tingling, or numbness (paresthesia) character-istic of nerve irritation. There can also be an electrical sensation radiating into the described part of the hand when the nerve is tapped over the site of entrapment (Tinel's sign). The usual location of the entrapment is about two-and-a-half inches up the forearm from the first extensor compartment. At this site, the sensory branch of the radial nerve emerges from between two forearm tendons to reach the skin. When the hand is pronated (turned palm downward), the two tendons "scissor" and can cause nerve compression. The combination of pronation and ulnar deviation can be particularly irritating. Affected musicians in-clude string players playing up-bow near the frog and pianists playing arpeggios, passing the thumb under the hand. Tight

71

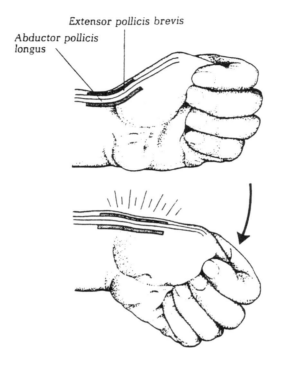

Extensor pollicis brevis

Abductor pollicis longus

Figure 3
The Finklestein test

Reprinted from *The Hand: Examination and Diagnosis*, 2d ed., 1983. By permission of the American Society for Surgery of the Hand.

watchbands or bracelets can aggravate the condition. In fact, this specific nerve compression is sometimes described in medical textbooks as "handcuff neuropathy," and musicians are well-advised to avoid having to have these devices applied!

Treatment

The treatment of de Quervain's disease consists primarily of adequate immobilization of the thumb in a thumb spica splint that goes from the tip of the thumb to about halfway up the forearm (Fig. 4). This splint can be custom-made by a hand therapist; the "Freedom" wrist/thumb spica splint can be purchased from

AliMed®, Inc.
297 High St.
Dedham, MA 02026
(800) 225-2610

A doctor's prescription is usually required. The splint should be removed every thirty to sixty minutes for a few minutes of pain-free, range-of-motion exercises. Prolonged, uninterrupted use of the splint can result in stiffness and increased symptomatology. While some weakness can occur as a result of splinting, protection, and allowing only gentle, controlled movements, there is little need for excessive concern. In most healthy people, strength will return in a relatively short time upon resumption of normal daily and musical activities. Of far greater concern is aggravating the injury by prematurely commencing resistive (strengthening) exercises prior to the diminution of pain. The use of therapy putty is a common offender in this circumstance.

If a splint cannot be tolerated or complied with, a padded fiber-glass cast can be used for a week or two, but will cause more stiffness than a removable splint. Both the splint and the cast should be "bubbled out" or "relieved" directly over the painful compartment to avoid direct, mechanical irritation of the tendons. In addition, the thumb must be aligned with the edge of the forearm (slight ulnar deviation) so that the thumb extensor

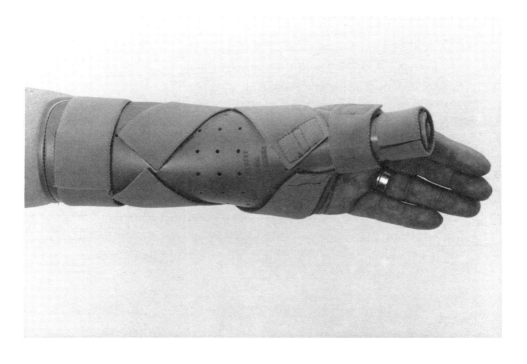

Figure 4
Thumb spica splint

Photo courtesy of AliMed; reprinted by permission.

tendons are placed in a straight line, the position of least tension. If pain persists, one or two cortisone injections can be helpful. Oral anti-inflammatory medications can also be a useful adjunct to treatment, but should not be used as the sole treatment without splinting. The advice of a physician should be obtained before taking these medications. An average dose of ibuprofen (a typical anti-inflammatory) would be 400 to 800 milligrams three times a day, taken with food. If pain persists despite six to eight weeks of treatment, or if the condition becomes chronic, then a relatively simple surgical procedure may be indicated to release the tight tunnel and free the tendons. Accessory tendons or multiple compartments must be sought during the procedure, because incomplete decompression will result in continued symptoms. A potential serious complication is inadvertent cutting of the sensory branch of the radial nerve, causing subsequent chronic pain or loss of sensation. Careful identification and protection of this nerve will prevent damage during surgery. The performer can anticipate returning to practice within two to three weeks after surgery, and to a full playing schedule another three to four weeks after that.

Summary

De Quervain's tendinitis is often preventable by minimizing stressful, sustained, or repetitive wrist positions. As usual, early recognition and appropriate treatment can head disability off at the pass.

Suggested Reading

Fry HJH. Overuse syndrome in clarinetists. *The Clarinet* 1987 Spring; 14(3): 48-50.

Mandel S; Patterson S; Johnson C. Overuse syndrome in a double bass player. *Medical Problems of Performing Artists* 1986 Dec; 1(4): 133-34.

Markison RE. Treatment of musical hands: redesign of the interface. *Hand Clinics* 1990 Aug; 6(3): 525-44.

Nolan WB; Eaton RG. Thumb problems of professional musicians. *Medical Problems of Performing Artists* 1989 Mar; 4(1): 20-24.

Shulman I; Milberg P. English horn player's thumb. [letter] *Journal of Hand Surgery* 1982 Jul; 7(4): 424.

Stern PJ. Tendinitis, overuse syndrome, and tendon injuries. *Hand Clinics* 1990 Aug; 6(3): 467-76.

Chapter 10

Problems of Flutists

To borrow a phrase from the computer vocabulary, the flute is not one of the most "user-friendly" instruments! There are numerous joint, muscle, and nerve problems that occur in flutists. In my medical practice and as an amateur flutist, I am well aware of the physical (and emotional) stresses and strains of playing the instrument. While I generally advocate physical conditioning exercises, there are also ways to adapt the instrument to make it more "friendly," or ergonomic. When a worker is out with an injury it costs the employer a great deal of money in worker's compensation. Therefore, many workplace tools have been redesigned to protect employees from injury. But when a musician is out with an injury, it often costs only the musician, so there has not been the same kind of effort put into redesigning instruments as has been put into redesigning tools.

The neck is a common area of dysfunction. The tilted and rotated head position has been around as long as the traverso. Just look at the drawing of Hotteterre (Fig. 1). The length of the flute necessitates rotating the head in order to relieve strain in the left shoulder. If the flute is then held parallel to the ground (Fig. 2), there is only rotation of the head, without tilt. However, the right arm must then be held up away from the body so that the fingers can stay in line with the wrist. This position strains the right shoulder, which is fatigued by the sustained contraction, and strains the neck muscles on the right side, because they contract to help stabilize the shoulder girdle. There is no way to hold the arm up away from the body and still have a relaxed shoulder. Many players compensate by dropping the right elbow down towards the body, thus relaxing the right shoulder muscles and perhaps increasing right-hand dexterity (Fig. 3). The resulting angulation of the instrument usually results in having to tilt the head 30° or 40°. Many teachers advise their students to "split the difference" and allow for a slight amount of head tilt and a slight dropping of the right elbow. This compromise is about the best we can do under the circumstances!

Both rotating and tilting the head are problematic. Wind instrumentalists ideally would like to play with the throat and neck muscles relaxed, whereas rotating and tilting the head requires neck-muscle contraction. Maintaining this position several hours a day for years can lead to imbalances in muscle strength and flexibility of the neck. This position also causes a mechanical narrowing of the openings (foramina) between the vertebrae where the spinal nerves exit (Fig. 4). When compounded by arthritic bone spurs (osteophytes), rotation and tilting can lead to nerve impingement (compression), causing symptoms ranging from neck and arm pain to numbness and tingling in the hand, mimicking carpal tunnel syndrome. This is termed *radiculitis* or *radiculopathy*, indicating irritation of the nerve roots in the neck as they exit through the cervical (neck) vertebrae. The neck is also very vulnerable to the muscle spasm of whiplash from automotive injuries, which may cause such discomfort upon rotation and tilting as to make playing the flute impossible.

A new design for the head joint has been developed by Emerson Musical Instruments under my direction (Fig. 5). By forming a 30° bend just past the lip plate, the angled head joint allows the head to remain in a nearly neutral position and still allows the right shoulder to be down in a relaxed position. The tone of the flute does not seem to be affected, but no formal testing has been done yet.

The angled head joint is available in both a student model and a solid silver model with a hand-cut embouchure. The angled head joint can increase comfort and decrease some of the physical problems of flute playing. One drawback to the design is a slight loss in stability of the instrument; enhanced stability can be achieved by use of a thumb rest.

Figure 1
Hotteterre

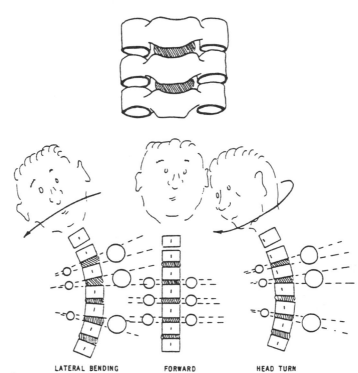

LATERAL BENDING   FORWARD   HEAD TURN

Figure 4
Narrowing of the openings (foramina) between the vertebrae

Reprinted from *Neck Pain*, 2d ed. Philadelphia: F.A. Davis Company, 1981; by permission
of Dr. Rene Cailliet and F.A. Davis Company.

Figure 2
With the flute held horizontally, there is increased tension in both the shoulders and left forearm extensors and increased pressure in the left carpal tunnel.

Figure 3
Shoulders and wrist are now relaxed, but neck muscles are tense and nerve foramina in cervical spine are narrowed on the right side.

Figure 5
Wrist and shoulders still relaxed. Head tilted only 10°, with minimal tension in neck.

Ergonomic Design for a Thumb Rest
and Finger Rest for the Flute

Although left-hand problems outnumber right-hand problems in flutists, there are quite a few flutists who have suffered from strain and physical tension in the base of the right thumb and surrounding musculature. While one could argue that this most likely represents an error of technique, with the person using an excessive amount of tension in the right hand, I believe the development of an ergonomically designed right thumb rest is indicated. I will describe what I believe to be an improved design based on the principles of physical analysis and structure of the hand. A rest for the left index finger will also be described.

The Right Thumb Rest

There is great variation in the position of the right thumb on the flute. Most commonly, the thumb is held underneath the flute and serves several functions. The first function of the right thumb is to support part of the weight of the flute.

The second is to provide opposition for the fingers as they press down on the keys. Because the point of support (approximately the baseline of the nail) is about one-and-a-half to two inches away from the muscles and ligaments at the base of the thumb, the thumb acts as a lever arm for the weight of the flute, while the base of the thumb acts as the fulcrum. In other words, the harder the flutist presses, the more force he or she transmits to the base of the thumb. The load is greater with the longer B-foot, gold, or platinum flutes. Leaky keys, which require increased force to seal, can also lead to increased force on the right thumb.

The third function of the right thumb is to stabilize the flute while playing notes in open position (no fingers down), such as C#, by squeezing the flute between the pinkie and the thumb of the right hand. The flute tends to be unstable in open positions because the mechanical rods on which the keys pivot are offset; that is, the rods fall outside the base of support of the right thumb, and therefore, when the fingers are lifted off the keys, the flute tends to roll in towards the player (Fig. 6). This rolling is usually counteracted by slightly increasing the pressure between the flute and the chin with the left hand, while squeezing the flute between the thumb and little finger of the right hand, creating a source of muscular tension in the right hand.

Another source of discomfort arises from the very small area of contact between the edge of the thumb and the rounded flute when the hand is held in the "natural" position (the side of the thumb facing the underside of the index finger—the position the thumb falls into when the hand is relaxed). This "natural" position concentrates the force from the flute over a small area of the thumb, which by its bony nature is not very pressure-tolerant (Fig. 7). The common solution to this problem is to rotate the thumb upward (supinate) so that the soft pad contacts the flute. This, however, is an unnatural position in that it requires muscular force to achieve and maintain. Increased muscular tension in the thumb and hand may cause not only pain and injury, but inhibition of maximal dexterity as well.

The Bo-pep thumb guide corrects some, but not all, of these mechanical problems. Regarding the contact area between the right thumb and the flute, the Bo-pep transforms the base of the flute from a convex surface into a concave one, more nearly conforming to the shape of the thumb and increasing the distribution of force over a wider surface area of the thumb. However, even with the Bo-pep, the weight of the mechanism rods still falls outside the base of support of the thumb, and the flute still tends to roll inward during open positions.

The device I have developed (StediRest) uses a nonslip, cork-lined metal clip that grips the flute and has an adjustable, foam-padded metal extension custom-fitted to the thumb (Figs. 8, 9). This device serves two main purposes: first, to distribute the pressure from the flute over a wider area of the thumb, allowing the thumb to be held comfortably in the "natural" position; second, to distribute the weight of the rods *through* the

Flute Cross Section and Right Hand

Figure 6

The weight of the
mechanism rods (arrow)
falls outside the base of
support (line B), which
causes the flute to tend to
roll inward with open
positions. Inward rolling
can be resisted by gripping
with the right thumb and
pinkie and/or pressing
harder against the jaw with
the left hand.

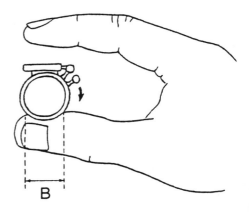

Figure 7

The area of thumb contact
with the flute (line B) is
quite bony and,
consequently, not very
pressure-tolerant.

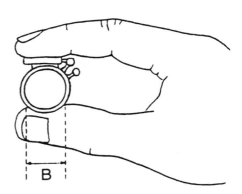

Figure 8

With the right-hand
StediRest, pressure from the
flute is distributed over a
wider area and the
mechanism's weight falls
within the base of support
(line B).

Figures 6, 7, and 8 by Ken Ishii
© 1993

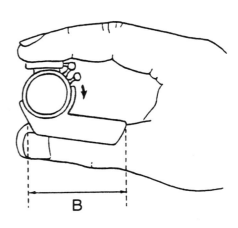

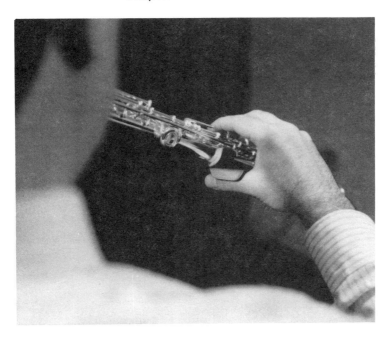

Figure 9 *(above) The right-hand StediRest*

Figure 10 *(below) The left-hand StediRest , wrapping around the base of the left index finger*

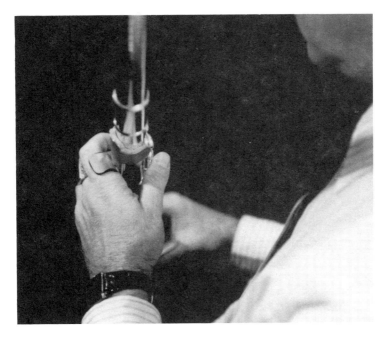

Figure 11
With the use of these rests, the flute can be easily
supported even without pressing down on the keys or
pressing the flute against the jaw.

base of support, stabilizing the flute by preventing it from rolling inwards.

The Left Index Rest

Typically, the left index finger is hyperextended at the knuckle joint, and the flute is supported on the ledge that is formed. In this position, compression of the nerve in the index finger is quite common, resulting in numbness, tingling, and/or pain. Furthermore, for the majority of flutists who lower the end of the flute to relax the right shoulder, the flute must be pressed by the base of the index finger rather firmly against the lower lip to prevent slipping of the instrument from the force of gravity. Interestingly, the two most common oral/dental problems of flutists are loosening of the lower teeth and temporomandibular joint (TMJ) pain. Both of these problems are apt to be related to the amount of pressure against the lower lip and teeth. The Bo-pep increases comfort by changing the rounded surface of the flute to fit the finger better, but does little to stabilize the instrument.

The left-hand StediRest utilizes a foam-padded hook that curls around the base of the left index finger, yielding both comfort and enhanced stability without increased pressure or muscular effort (Fig. 10). For the first time, the flute can be completely supported and stabilized from below without using any fingers on top or excessive pressure inward against the jaw (Fig. 11). This should not only aid in the prevention of injury, but also enhance finger dexterity because the hands are more relaxed.

The StediRests are available from

> Performance Ergonomics
> Kyle Scott, President
> 3533 Covered Bridge Lane
> Lakeridge, VA 22192

Portions of this chapter were adapted from articles by Dr. Norris that appeared in *Medical Problems of Performing Artists*, © December 1990, Hanley & Belfus, Philadelphia, and *Flutist Quarterly*, Summer 1989. Reprinted by permission.

Chapter 11

The "Lazy Finger" Syndrome: Tendon Variations of the Pinkie

Not long ago, a violin student came to me complaining of pain in the forearm along the pinkie side from the wrist to the elbow. She had been practicing a new piece with a lot of double-stops. She had had some difficulty with this, and her teacher constantly chided her about her pinkie being a "lazy finger." She followed his advice to work harder, and the result was forearm pain. Because tendinitis or muscle strain often develops when one begins unfamiliar or unusually intense musical activity, it would have been easy to assume that this was the cause of her injury. However, I had recently read an article in the *Journal of Hand Surgery* stating that up to forty per cent of the general population has an anatomic variation in which the flexor tendons (the tendons that curl the fingers in towards the palm) of the ring finger and pinkie are joined together in varying degrees in the region of the wrist and/or forearm by tendinous interconnections (Fig. 1). This actually represents a failure to separate during embryological development, as the tendons originate as a single block of tissue. Occasionally, the middle finger is also interconnected to the ring finger. Recalling this article, I performed the simple clinical test (Fig. 2) to determine whether or not my violinist patient had tendinous interconnections. She did. Since that time, I have had numerous occasions to diagnose this condition. While it can occur in either hand or both, it usually is symptomatic only when occurring in the left hands of string players and guitarists. In the right hand, the variation is of little or no consequence. All string and guitar teachers should learn how to perform this simple test so as to avoid the error of regarding a tendinous interconnection as a "lazy finger," and thus spare their students pain and suffering.

What is the significance of this anatomic variation for musicians? When playing a string instrument, the ring finger and pinkie are often required to separate; for example, during double-stops or little-finger slides. If tendinous interconnections are present, these two fingers always tend to stay together—the ring finger always tries to follow the pinkie. Attempting to force the fingers apart, as when playing double-stops on a violin, or large chords on a guitar, causes mechanical stress and, therefore, pain. This pain is characteristically located along the ulnar border of the flexor side of the forearm (the part of the forearm that rests on the table when holding a drinking glass). The resulting soreness can be alleviated by massage, gentle stretching and strengthening exercises, ice massage, other therapeutic modalities, and reducing manual activities (musical and nonmusical). However, unless the underlying cause is identified, the condition will recur, resulting in a cycle of pain and frustration.

How can this syndrome be treated? The tendinous interconnection is often so dense or extensive that it cannot be stretched out. Surgical separation is possible, but success is unpredictable. What can be done is to analyze the player's repertoire for passages that require wide separation of the ring finger and pinkie. Whenever possible, refingering those passages so that the ring finger and pinkie are not at odds with each other can alleviate strain. When the passage cannot be refingered, the player should avoid repetitious practice of it in order to minimize the risk of injury.

Discussion of the "lazy finger" syndrome raises another issue: should string teachers screen new students for this condition, just as aspiring ballet students are screened for their ability to "turn out" at the hips? While not a predictor of certain failure, "lazy finger" syndrome does make playing more difficult; awareness from the outset that the condition is present may be useful for teachers and students.

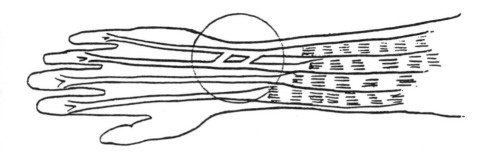

Figure 1
A schematic representation of the tendinous interconnections
between the ring finger and pinkie

After Kalus, *Medical Problems of Performing Artists* 1987 June; 2(2): 58.

Figure 2: (facing page)
A simple clinical test for tendinous interconnections

When the index, middle, and ring fingers are restrained in full extension, the ability to flex the pinkie at the first finger knuckle (PIP joint) demonstrates an independent flexor tendon.

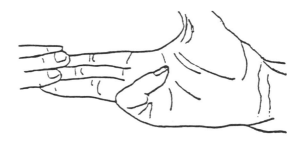

The inability to flex the pinkie at the PIP joint with the others restrained indicates tendinous interconnections between the ring finger and pinkie. The examiner feels the ring finger trying to flex along with the pinkie.

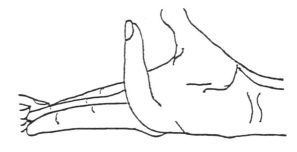

Releasing the ring finger now allows both to flex freely at the PIP joint. If there is still resistance, and if easy PIP flexion of the ring finger and pinkie can only be attained with release of the middle finger, this indicates tendinous interconnections among all three.

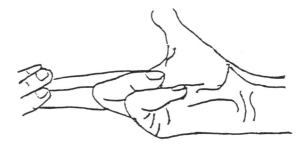

Chapter 12

Focal Dystonia (Occupational Cramp)

Focal dystonia, also referred to in the medical literature as occupational cramp (the terms will be used here interchangeably), is one of the most puzzling and distressing conditions for both performers and those who treat their disorders. Fortunately, it is uncommon, comprising less than one per cent of the hundreds of musician patients I have seen. This figure generally agrees with reports from other centers (Lederman).

Focal dystonia usually presents as painless incoordination or loss of voluntary motor control of highly skilled movement. This almost invariably affects intensive professional activity, the most frequent example being writer's cramp. Occupational cramps have been recognized for about 250 years and were first reported in musicians about 150 years ago.

According to Wilson, there are multiple risk factors that may interact in very complicated ways in an individual to result in focal dystonia. In the majority of cases, electrodiagnostic testing (EMG/NCV) does not reveal abnormalities indicative of nerve or muscle damage, although subtle nerve entrapments may be involved on occasion. An EMG performed using surface electrodes to show muscle activity may reveal abnormalities of contraction patterns. Normally, the muscle or motor system is designed so that when one muscle group contracts, the muscles on the other side of the joint automatically relax, so that the limb or body part may move freely. This is referred to physiologically as *reciprocal inhibition*. Simultaneous contraction of muscles on either side of a joint is called *co-contraction*, and makes joint movement difficult or impossible. Sometimes, of course, we co-contract on purpose, to stabilize a joint during certain types of activities. In occupational cramp, however, co-contraction is an unwanted occurrence that impedes performance by increasing resistance to intentional movement. Special electrodiagnostic testing (long latency reflex) shows co-contractions and failure of reciprocal inhibition.

Music-making is probably the most complex of all human neuromuscular activities. Musicians have to play with great rapidity and accuracy. Wilson notes that musicians operate the nervous system at or close to the limits of its functional capacity. When the extreme subtleties of motor control that we call "expressiveness" are considered, the demands are even more remarkable. After all, two players can play the same virtuoso passage at the same tempo and one will move us to tears while the other seems mechanical. Ultimately, the differences come down to subtleties of motor control! It seems to me that spending years repeating highly complex motor skills for long hours (with playing music representing the pinnacle) is a very recent activity from an evolutionary standpoint. Perhaps people who develop occupational cramps are "bumping up" against the limits of their nervous systems, just as athletes confront limits of their musculoskeletal systems.

Focal dystonia is usually associated with intense and prolonged practice of complex actions and is uncommon in amateurs or in people who have been playing only a few years. It has been reported in typists working at high speeds for long hours and years. (I certainly don't have to worry about developing it!) It is often associated with a precipitating factor, such as a change in instrument or technique, or obsessive practice in the attempt to increase the speed of a difficult or awkward passage. Actual injury, either acute trauma or overuse, may precede focal dystonia.

There have been reports of a secondary type of focal dystonia associated with subtle entrapment or compression of various nerves in the hand or forearm (Charness). However, releasing these nerves surgically often fails to resolve the dystonic symptoms. Wilson also cites the work of Christoph Wagner in Germany regarding certain biomechanical factors that may predispose to developing occupational cramp: for example, reduced passive abduction (spreading apart) of the fingers and limited supination (rotation) of the forearms.

As with writer's cramp, musician's cramp often starts out being task-specific, occurring only while the person is playing the instrument. For string players, this most often appears as a loss of control (either curling or straightening) of the ring finger and pinkie of the left hand, although the bow arm has also been reported to be affected (Lederman). I have also seen focal dystonia develop in the left trapezius (the back muscle between the base of the neck and the shoulder) of a cellist who had previously had a traumatic injury to her left hand and, as a result, had to alter her technique. With time, the cramp often progresses and generalizes to other, non-musical movements, eventually interfering with daily activities.

Interestingly, in pianists, the cramp shows up most often in the ring finger and pinkie of the right hand, which has a greater demand on its agility while it "labors under the disadvantage of lighter and thinner strings" (Hochberg et al.). This problem was experienced by both Gary Graffman and Leon Fleisher, eventually ending their performance careers except for the few pieces for left hand alone. I believe that this predilection for the ring finger and pinkie to experience dystonia may be explained on an anatomical and neurological basis. The thumb, index, and middle fingers are designed for fine motor control and manipulation. The ring finger and pinkie are the power-grip part of the hand. Their metacarpals, being more mobile in flexion, are designed to close down powerfully around an object (Tubiana). They are not designed for the prolonged, rapid, highly complex and coordinated movements demanded in musical performance. Apparently, they are sometimes just not up to the demanding task of intense music-making, neurologically speaking, and go "on the fritz"! Some neurologists (Lederman and Hallet) do not report this specificity for ring finger and pinkie flexion among their patients, citing a great variability of finger, wrist, and forearm involvement.

Also interesting is that occupational cramp is seen in the embouchure muscles of wind instrumentalists and the vocal cord muscles of singers (spastic dysphonia), muscles that are called upon to make rapid, minute changes for long, intense periods of time.

The development of focal dystonia can be psychologically devastating to the performer who is accustomed to a high degree of control over his or her body. "If the person, alarmed and confused, further intensifies his or her efforts, the problem always gets worse" (Wilson). Often, there is reluctance to seek medical care or advice, as Graffman has pointed out.

Rest, even for prolonged periods, has not proved particularly helpful. However, the musician should play only as part of a retraining program, since repetition of abnormal movement only tends to stabilize the abnormality (Wilson). Biofeedback and strengthening exercises have not proved successful.

Attempts to weaken the involuntary muscle contraction by injecting botulinum toxin (Botox) into the affected muscles have had only limited success, primarily in preventing the hand from becoming incapacitated for daily use, not in restoring lost musical facility. Most of this research has been done at the National Institute of Health (NIH) in Bethesda, MD, by Hallett and associates. The toxin is produced by *Clostridium bacillus* and is the same one that causes food poisoning. The involved muscles are first identified by sophisticated electrical testing and then the toxin is injected in tiny doses, given about two weeks apart. The toxin acts by blocking nerve impulses to the muscle; its effects last about three months or longer. The injection may need to be repeated. The challenge is to use enough Botox to decrease the spasm, but not so much as to cause muscle weakness, the most common side effect. This is still an experimental technique and available at only a few medical research centers. Patients may develop potentially serious allergic reactions to the toxin (Calne).

Perhaps the most encouraging approach to treatment so far has been technical retraining by certain teachers. One of the chief difficulties is that a medical diagnosis of dystonia was not made prior to the few reported cases of success. Neuromuscular re-education via Alexander Technique or Feldenkrais "Awareness Through Movement" may be especially valuable in this regard, but the studies simply haven't been done yet and we are left, for the time being, with anecdotes. Interestingly, Gowers (one of the great early neurologists, writing about occupational writer's cramp in the 1880's) stressed the importance of changing writing technique as treatment for the condition. According to Calne, Gowers's patients who switched from right-handed to left-handed writing went on to develop the cramp in the left hand. This has also been observed in a violinist with left-hand dystonia who switched to fingering with the right hand only to develop the dystonia in the right hand. Very interesting!

According to Wilson, the process of stabilization of skilled movement, both normal and abnormal, remains poorly understood. And while it's frustrating that we still lack a good definition of, let alone treatment for, focal dystonia, there are people working hard to gain a better understanding of just how the nervous system functions in music-making. It is my hope and anticipation that increased understanding will lead to improved ability to treat and ultimately prevent this singular disorder.

Note: The author is indebted to Frank Wilson, M.D., neurologist, music medicine specialist (UCSF/Kaiser), researcher, author, and avid amateur musician, for generously sharing his time and views regarding focal dystonia.

References

Calne, D. The nature and treatment of dystonias. Paper presented at the 5th Annual Conference on Medical Problems of Musicians and Dancers. Aspen: 1987.

Graffman, G. Doctor, can you lend an ear? *Medical Problems of Performing Artists* 1986 Mar; 1(1): 3-6.

Tubiana, R. *Examination of the Hand.* Philadelphia: WB Saunders, 1984.

Wagner, C. Success and failure in musical performance: biomechanics of the hand. In: *The Biology of Music Making: Proceedings of the 1984 Denver Conference.* Roehman and Wilson, eds. St. Louis: MMB Music, 1988, 154-79.

Wilson, F. *Tone Deaf and All Thumbs.* New York: Vintage Books, 1986.

Suggested Reading

Cohen LG; Hallett M. Hand cramps: clinical features and electromyograhpic patterns in a focal dystonia. *Neurology* 1988; 38: 1005-12.

Cole RA; Cohen LG; Hallet M. Treatment of musician's cramp with botulinum toxin. *Medical Problems of Performing Artists* 1992 Dec; 6(4): 137-43.

Fry HJH; Hallett M. Focal dystonia (occupational cramp) masquerading as nerve entrapment or hysteria. *Plastic and Reconstructive Surgery* 1988 Nov; 82(5): 908-10.

Hochberg FH; Harris SU; Blattert TR. Occupational hand cramps: professional disorders of motor control. *Hand Clinics* 1990 Aug; 6(3): 417-28.

Hoppmann RA; O'Brien JB; Chodacki D; Chenier TC. Pseudoephedrine for focal dystonia. *Medical Problems of Performing Artists* 1991 Jun; 6(2): 48-50.

Lederman RJ. Focal dystonia in instrumentalists: clinical features. *Medical Problems of Performing Artists* 1991 Dec; 6(4): 132-36.

Lockwood AH. Focal dystonic movements provoked by use of the unaffected hand: mirror-movement dystonia. *Medical Problems of Performing Artists* 1992 Mar; 7(1): 22-24.

Merriman L; Newmark J; Hochberg FH; Shahani B; Leffert R. A focal movement disorder of the hand in six pianists. *Medical Problems of Performing Artists* 1986 Mar; 1(1): 17-19.

Newmark J; Hochberg FH. Isolated painless manual incoordination in 57 musicians. *Journal of Neurology, Neurosurgery and Psychiatry* 1987 Mar; 50(3): 291-95.

Chapter 13

Therapeutic Exercise for Musicians

Physical exercise plays a vital role in keeping performers fit and healthy. Making music, while not athletics in the strict sense of the word, definitely has physical aspects. The body is an integral part of one's instrument (and for vocalists, the instrument itself). Muscles that are tight, weak, or poorly conditioned are hardly ideal vehicles for inspired musical expression, and are often a source of physical discomfort that can be distracting at least and disabling at worst.

Many musicians are interested in exercise; however, there is often confusion as to what is the best or proper type to do. This chapter will attempt to guide the performer towards a comprehensive, balanced program of exercise. Like a balanced diet, an exercise program should have several components: strength, flexibility, and endurance. Ideally, a musician should have a routine that does not entail expensive equipment or memberships and that can be done in an apartment or hotel room without disturbing the neighbors! Let's look at the components in more detail.

Flexibility

Stretching muscles and tendons increases the blood flow and prepares them for physical activity. The chief component of muscle and connective tissue is collagen. Collagen is contractile, like elastic. If allowed to remain in a shortened position for long periods, it becomes tight, restricting free movement. Like elastic, it stretches most easily when warm, and therefore, stretching is best done after a hot shower or some mild exercise to gently raise body temperature. Stretches should be slow and sustained: at least thirty to sixty seconds, and longer for tighter or larger muscles. Stretching should be done only to the point of moderate discomfort, not to the point of pain, or there is a risk of tearing instead of stretching. All the muscles of the body, not just the hands or fingers, should be stretched. It's a good idea to do at least one good stretching session early in the day and then to repeat it, perhaps more briefly, before and after practice. Stretching may also be combined with slow deep-breathing exercises. Yoga classes are readily available and affordable at many "Y's" or community centers. Many excellent books on stretching can be found in the health section of bookstores. The paperback *You Are Your Instrument* by Julie Lyonn Lieberman is a good one and may be ordered from

P.O. Box 495
New York, NY 10024-3202

We should also consider the concept of instrument-specific stretches. For example, the flutist usually rotates the head to the left and tilts it to the right. This can cause imbalances over the course of months or years. The flutist needs to emphasize the opposite movements in a stretching program. Likewise, the violist's left shoulder is always externally rotated and the bow-arm somewhat internally rotated, so working on opposite stretches will help avoid imbalances. The harpist's spine is usually rotated to the left because the left hand must reach forward to play the bass strings. The harpist needs to work on spine rotation to the right, and so on.

Strength

One needn't be a Stallone or Schwarzenegger to play the fiddle, but a certain modicum of strength and muscle tone is desirable to help prevent fatigue and injury. This is particularly true of the larger instruments and for persons of small stature. Backs and muscles can be strained by carrying the instrument as readily as by playing it! When possible, heavier instruments should be transported in cases with wheels or on folding airline-luggage dollies. Swimming is excellent for both strength and endurance, but is often expensive or difficult to fit into a busy schedule. A good toning program can be accomplished easily and inexpensively by the use of Thera-band, a broad elastic strip available in different colors, each a different grade of resistance. It comes in six-yard rolls for about $8 from Rolyan:

> Ph.: (800) 558-8633
> catalog number: A521-7 (medium resistance) or
> A521-8 (heavy resistance)

Rolyan sells books of exercises also, but you can quite easily make up your own. You can cut the roll into one- or two-yard pieces and either hold each end or roll the ends around a short piece of broomstick or dowel.

Endurance

Physical stamina is probably more critical for some instruments than others, but is certainly an important component of health for everyone. One may alternate the various components of the exercise program, but most experts recommend at least twenty minutes of strenuous exercise three or four times per week. Persons who have health problems, are over forty, or have not regularly engaged in strenuous exercise should check with their physicians before starting an exercise program. My favorite exercise program is non-impact aerobics, which is largely based on dance and martial arts movements and can be done in a small area without making much noise. There is an excellent and inexpensive video called "NIA" by Debbie and Carlos Rosas available from Vestron, Inc., Stamford, CT, or video stores. T'ai chi is also excellent exercise, and when done briskly over twenty or thirty minutes, can afford a good workout that is both stimulating and relaxing. Classes are usually easily found and inexpensive.

I have recently produced a one-hour videotape (VHS) covering and demonstrating all aspects of a musician's exercise program. The tape, "Therapeutic Exercise for Musicians," was made of my presentation at the 1990 "Playing (less) Hurt"[©] conference on music medicine in Minneapolis. The video is based on the material I developed for my course "Physical Education for Musicians" at the New England Conservatory. The exercises are drawn and blended from more than twenty years of study and practice of yoga, T'ai chi, and dance, and from my medical background in physical rehabilitation and orthopedics. The tape may be ordered for $35 (US) by check or credit card from

> MMB Music Co., Inc.
> 10370 Page Industrial Blvd.
> St. Louis, MO 63132
> Ph.: (800) 543-3771

This chapter originally appeared in *Senza Sordino* 1990 June and is reprinted by permission.

Suggested Reading

Bosanquet RC. The Alexander principle and its importance to music education. *British Journal of Music Education* 1987; 4(3): 229-42.

Grindea C., ed. *Tension in the Performance of Music.* 2d ed. London: Kahn & Averill, 1988.

Heggie J; Rose E. Awareness through movement. *Instrumentalist* 1986 Apr; 40: 36-39.

Jerome J. The pleasures of stretching. *Strings* 1988 Summer; 3(1): 14-21.

Spell E. Posture: quick tips for flutists: part I. *Flutist Quarterly* 1986 Spring; 11(3): 52-53.

Chapter 14

Returning to Play After Injury

The treatment of injury really has two distinct, although overlapping, phases. Reducing pain or symptoms by the various means discussed in previous chapters represents only the first stage. If the player has had to stop or significantly reduce playing during the healing phase, a graduated, methodical plan for returning to full musical and daily activities is essential to avoid emotionally and physically distressing relapses. In the field of occupational medicine, this concept is called *work hardening* or *work conditioning*. The worker performs his or her specific tasks, but starts out at a greatly reduced level of time and intensity. The process of gradually building up to normal activity is usually guided or supervised by a physical or occupational therapist. For both functional and psychological reasons, the workplace is ideal for work hardening. For the orchestral musician, however, there are often obstacles to this. A player often needs a doctor's note to miss work because of an injury, but does not usually need authorization to return to work. This frequently leads to premature return and relapse, especially if the player has not undergone a work hardening (shall we call this *play hardening*?) program. When a player returns to work on a part-time basis, there is often resistance from fellow orchestra members, who feel resentful or envious that the injured player is afforded an easier schedule. This should be counteracted by educating the other musicians about the necessity for a gradual return to work after an injury.

Injured musicians usually miss playing so much, and often have so much anxiety about being away from their instruments, that as soon as they start to feel somewhat recovered, they attempt to leap prematurely back to their usual routine, often with disastrous consequences. Fry quotes Poore (1887) on this:

> Treatment: The most important point in treatment is rest. The excessive use of the hand must be discontinued, and it is often necessary to insist on this rather forcibly. Piano playing, if not prohibited altogether, must only be practiced to a degree short of that which causes pain or annoyance. It is often difficult to restrain the ardor of these patients in the matter of playing. Directly they feel in a small degree better, they fly to the piano; and I have known the progress of more than one case very seriously retarded by the undoing, as it were, of the good effect of rest by an hour's injudicious and prohibited "practising."

These words, written over one hundred years ago, show that things have not changed much! Ideally, the treating physician or therapist will devote ample time to counseling the patient in avoiding this common error and in exercising patience, restraint, and good judgment while recovering. As the Chinese saying goes, "The wise horse runs at the shadow of the whip," and it is indeed a wise patient who is able to learn by the mistakes of others and needn't feel the pain of the "whip" in his very bones in order to learn his lesson! Patients should be reassured that they are not going to lose their "chops" in a few weeks, and that instead of feeling like they're serving time in the "penalty box," they can put their time to good use by working on music theory, harmony, sight-reading or *solfège*, critically listening to recordings, or learning something about the business aspects of music and career promotion.

Now to some specifics. In the first place, it is not always necessary to stop playing entirely. Often, reducing the intensity and/or time of playing, choosing an easier repertoire, or taking more frequent breaks may suffice. If the left hand is injured, one can sometimes continue to do bow work or right-hand keyboard work. If the right hand is injured, one can work on fingering. Nor is it necessary to be completely asymptomatic before beginning the work-conditioning program. A person who is not yet ready or able to deal with the physical instrument can go through the motions of playing without the instrument—what Menuhin refers to as "shadow playing." In fact, I often recommend that the recovering player be able to shadow-play comfortably for several minutes prior to beginning on the instrument.

When the person is ready to return to the instrument, I will review a detailed "return to playing" schedule with him or her. I feel it is inadequate and inappropriate for a physician merely to advise the player who is ready to return to playing to "go back little by little." This is too vague and open to misinterpretation. The value of a written schedule is that it minimizes the risk of overdoing. Players must be advised to adhere to the schedule even if they feel that they can do more. The use of a clock or timer is helpful. The problem is that one often does not feel when one is overdoing it at the time of activity. The pain evolves several hours later. Anyone who has gone skiing or horseback riding for the first time in a long time knows that after the joy of a whole day's activity, the "charley horse" follows the next day!

I will usually recommend starting with five minutes once or twice a day, but if the injury was severe or the person has had to take off for a long time, he or she might begin cautiously with a single two- or three-minute period and see how the injury feels later on or the next day. A brief physical warmup (see chapter 13) should precede and follow playing, and if there is still some pain or discomfort, the sore part may be iced down for ten minutes or so after the playing session.

The accompanying illustration is a sample schedule I have devised (Fig. 1). It is not scientifically based and represents only one of several possible ways to accomplish return to playing. The schedule can and should be modified to suit the individual player. In addition to the warmup and cooldown, one should begin with slow, easy pieces or études. I often recommend using a metronome at a medium setting and gradually working up to faster tempos by clicking up a notch or two every few days. One should also gradually work down towards slower tempos, as the control required to play very slowly can be demanding as well. As the work hardening progresses, the player gradually resumes more technically difficult material.

The sample schedule is divided into play and rest periods. Each level represents a unit of time, usually from three to seven days, although this can be adjusted to meet individual needs. One should be comfortable at a given level before progressing to the next level, like a mountain climber acclimatizing at a given altitude before ascending to the next height. The play periods gradually increase with each level, while the rest periods gradually decrease. However, the play periods do not increase beyond about fifty minutes, and the rest periods do not fall below five or ten minutes. Again, if the injury has been severe, one would probably want to progress even more slowly than indicated in the given schedule. If pain reappears after progressing to the next level, one should drop back one or two levels until the symptoms subside. It may even be necessary to stop for a day or two before resuming playing. If one encounters difficulty in progressing, it may be necessary to do a mini-progression, changing only one vertical column every three or four days. For example, rather than increasing all the play and rest periods at a single time from level four to level five, the musician would increase only the first play period to level five, leaving the remainder of the play and rest periods at level four. After a few days, he or she would decrease the first rest period to level five, again leaving the remainder at level four. After a few more days, the second play period is increased, then the second rest period decreased, etc. In this fashion, one may be able to make steady, albeit slow, progress and avoid discouragement and depression. In the sample program, level ten represents about four hours of playing time. A performer who requires more than this would simply keep adding more play and rest periods, as shown, until achieving the desired goal.

Returning to Play

- Start with slow and easy pieces; gradually progress to faster, more difficult pieces.

- In general, maximum 50 minutes play with minimum 10 minutes rest.

- *Warm up* before playing!

Levels (3-7 Days Each)	Play	Rest	Play	Rest	Play	Play	Rest	Play	Rest
1	5	60	5						
2	10	50	10						
3	15	40	15	60	5				
4	20	30	20	50	10				
5	30	20	25	40	15	45	5		
6	35	15	35	30	20	35	10		
7	40	10	40	20	25	25	15	50	10
8	50	10	45	15	30	15	25	40	15
9	50	10	50	10	40	10	35	30	20
10	50	10	50	10	50	10	45	20	30
Etc.									

Figure 1

Markison astutely recommends recording one's practice periods and using the rest periods to critique what was just practiced. This permits a physical rest while remaining musically engaged with the practice session.

To avoid discouragement, the musician should be advised from the start that setbacks are to be expected. Taking three steps forward and one back is not unusual, given that one is trying to balance not increasing too quickly with not going too slowly. Following a graduated program minimizes the risk of overdoing: if the load is too much, it will be only a little too much and the setback will be small and recovery swift. To sum it up with another aphorism: Hasten slowly and you shall soon arrive!

Portions of this chapter from an article by Richard Norris that appeared in *Strings: The Magazine for Players and Makers of Bowed String Instruments.* San Anselmo, CA: String Letter Press, © 1991. Reprinted with permission.

Chapter 15

Stage Fright and the Use of Inderal

Every infection of the mind that is attended by hope or
fear is the cause of an agitation to the heart.
—*Dr. William Harvey, 1628*

Nearly every performer has experienced the discomfort of anxiety during performance—the "psychic demons stalking them on the stage" (Wilson). The causes of performance anxiety are varied and complex and beyond the scope of this discussion. We will focus on the use and abuse of beta blockers, of which the best known is Inderal (propranolol).

What Are Beta Blockers?

Beta blockers are a class of drugs that block the effects of adrenalin on the body. These effects include rapid heartbeat; sweaty palms; "butterflies" in the stomach; trembling hands; dry mouth; and rapid, shallow breathing. Adrenalin is released by the adrenal glands (so called because they are located on top of the kidneys) in response to real or perceived danger to survival of the organism—the "fight or flight" response. Unfortunately, in its extreme forms, this response interferes with music-making. Inderal and the other beta blockers prevent or minimize the body's response to adrenalin by being absorbed by the same receptor sites throughout the body as adrenalin, effectively blocking adrenalin's ability to be used. The principal medical uses of beta blockers are in treating high blood pressure, chest pains (angina), and certain types of irregular heartbeat (arrhythmias).

Beta Blockers and Performance Anxiety

The idea of using beta blockers to control performance anxiety was first reported in the British medical journal *Lancet* by James et al.in 1977 and in the U.S.A. by Brantigan and Brantigan in 1979. Since then, the use of Inderal has become widespread among both professionals and students, often without medical prescription. In the 1986 ICSOM survey (Fishbein et al.), nearly twenty-five per cent of players surveyed used Inderal on an occasional basis for performance anxiety, most without medical prescription.

While generally a safe, non-addictive medication, Inderal can have severe side effects, such as precipitating asthma attacks and heart failure in susceptible individuals. Lightheadedness, sleep disturbances, nausea, and diarrhea have also been reported. Thus, the medication should never be taken without medical supervision.

Although not formally approved by the FDA (Food and Drug Administration) for use in performance anxiety, Inderal is commonly prescribed for this purpose. It has marked advantages over alcohol or tranquilizers such as Valium, which act on the brain and have been known to cause both clumsy fingers and "lousy reviews."

When taken on an occasional basis and in the small doses required to prevent anxiety, the above-mentioned side effects are minimized. The usual dose for performance anxiety is twenty to forty milligrams by mouth, one to two hours before a performance. Since there is great variation in the way different people metabolize the medication, the dose may vary and should be individualized. A person should have one or more trials before using Inderal for a performance so as to avoid uncertainty regarding the effect of the drug.

Use and Abuse

When is it appropriate to consider the use of a beta blocker? The performing musician has chosen a career in which one's very personal artistic expressions are subjected to public scrutiny and criticism. While the risks inherent in playing before a live audience can be rewarding (even thrilling), the demands by today's musical public for flawless, virtuoso performances and the realities of ever-increasing numbers of talented young competitors can strain the limits of even the coolest psyche.

On the one hand, it may be very helpful to use a beta blocker before a major audition, recital, or exposed solo in order that the player have a positive experience and gain control over performance phobia. On the other hand, there are those who would say that learning to conquer performance anxiety is a prerequisite to artistic and personal maturity, which is part of the artist's necessary evolution, not to be "leapfrogged" with a pill (Gabbard).

Certainly, if a section player or soloist requires Inderal on a daily basis in order to do a gig, there is cause for concern, and an indication that the individual should be receiving psychological counseling. The combined Inderal/counseling strategy can help the musician gain control, possibly leading to a deeper insight into the sources of personal artistic and creative impulses (Wilson).

References

Brantigan, C.O., Brantigan, T.A. Effect of beta blockade and beta stimulation on stage fright. *The American Journal of Medicine* 1982 Jan; 72: 88-94.

Fishbein, M., Middlestadt, SE., et al. Medical problems among ICSOM musicians: overview of a national survey. *Medical Problems of Performing Artists* 1988 March; 3(1): 1-8.

Gabbard, GO. Stage fright: coping methods and formal treatments. *The Piano Quarterly* 1981 Summer; 15-20.

Neftel, KA, et al. Stage fright in musicians. *Psychosomatic Medicine* 1982 Nov; 44(5): 461-69.

Nies, AS. Clinical pharmacology of beta adrenergic blockers. *Medical Problems of Performing Artists* 1986 Mar; 1(1): 25-29.

Noyes, R. Beta-blocking drugs and anxiety. *Psychosomatics* 1982 Feb; 23(2): 155-70.

Rosenbaum, JF. The drug treatment of anxiety. *The New England Journal of Medicine* 1982 Feb 18; 306(7): 401.

Wilson, FR. Inderal for stage fright? *The Piano Quarterly* (134): 30-35.

Appendix A

MUSIC MEDICINE   SELF-HISTORY FORM

developed by Richard N.Norris, MD

Date:_____

Last name :_____   Date of birth:_____

First name:_____   Address (School):_____

Tel:_____   Address (Home) :_____

Affiliation or School:_____   semester:_____

Name address & tel of Family Doctor :._____

GENERAL MEDICAL HISTORY:

Are you presently under a doctor's care? Y/ N. For what?_____

Previous serious illness or injury? (Brief description)_____

Previous performance injury?_____

Taking any prescription medications? (name & dose)_____

PERFORMANCE HISTORY:

Instrument: Primary:_____   Secondary_____

# of years played_____   Status: student   profess.   amateur_____

 Dominant hand ? R   L

Approximate # of hours play/day ; before injury_____   now?_____   (since)_____

Frequency & duration of breaks ?_____

(Physical) warm up prior to play?_____   Regular physical exercise program?_____

Onset of problem:_____

113

Symptoms (What do you feel?) _____

Area of symptom or pain _____

Have you had to change technique or repertoire due to injury? Y N

Precipitating factor(s): rapid increase in : playing time technical difficulty

Change of : teacher styles instrument repertoire ?

Is carrying the instrument or equipment painful? Y N .

Previous treatment(s): medical chiropractic physical therapy

occupational therapy massage medication (which?) dosage

other What helped most? _____

What motions or activities makes it worse? _____

Are daily activities painful? Y N. Which? dressing kitchen writing

opening doors other Pain during sleep or on awakening? Y/N . (Stop here

please)

Upcoming performance committments? _____

Physical Examination : area of pain/sx _____

_____

AROM: _____ PROM _____

Muscle testing _____

Sensory/neuro _____ Technical comments _____

_____

Plan: PT___OT___ home program___MD Consultant___Radiology___other_____

Tests pending or ordered _____

Recheck in ___weeks. Follow up visits: _____

_____

_____

_____

Appendix B

Performing Arts Medicine Clinics

The following list of clinics was compiled from various journal, newsletter, and conference sources. It is intended for informational use only and does not imply any endorsement by the author. The clinics are listed alphabetically by state, followed by foreign clinics. Please note that some of these facilities are full-service clinics, while others are primarily referral services. For further information, please contact the specific clinic.

Southern California Arts Medicine Program
3413 W. Pacific Ave., Suite 204
Burbank, CA 91505
(818) 953-4430
Contact: Martha Paterson, Occupational Therapy

Department of Physical Medicine and Rehabilitation
Loma Linda University Medical Center
11234 Anderson St.
Loma Linda, CA 92354
(714) 799-2101
Director: Dr. Scott Brown

Performing Arts Medicine
Kaiser Permanente
7601 Stoneridge Dr.
Pleasanton, CA 94588
(510) 847-5282
Contact: Dr. Frank Wilson

Health Program for Performing Artists
San Francisco Medical Center
University of California
400 Parnassus Ave., 5th Floor
San Francisco, CA 94143
(415) 476-7373
Director: Dr. Peter Ostwald

115

University of Colorado Health Sciences Center
Department of Neurology
Campus Box B 183
4200 E. Ninth Ave.
Denver, CO 80262
(303) 270-7566
Contact: Dr. Stuart Schneck

Medical Program for Performing Artists
Rehabilitation Institute of Chicago
345 E. Superior St.
Chicago, IL 60611
(312) 908-ARTS
Director: Dr. Alice Brandfonbrener

Division of Performing Arts Medicine
Evanbrook Orthopaedic and Sports Medicine Associates, Ltd.
1144 Wilmette Ave.
Wilmette, IL 60201
(708) 853-9400
Director: Dr. William J. Dawson

Rebound Sports Medicine
839 Auto Mall Rd.
Bloomington, IN 47401
(812) 332-6200
Contact: Lexi Orfanos, Physical Therapy

Performing Arts Medicine Program
Indiana University School of Medicine
541 Clinical Dr.
Indianapolis, IN 46223
(317) 274-4225
Director: Dr. Kenneth D. Brandt

Music Medicine Clinic
Massachusetts General Hospital
1 Hawthorne Pl., Suite 103
Boston, MA 02114
(617) 726-8657
Director: Dr. Fred Hochberg

Performing Arts Clinic
Brigham and Women's Hospital
75 Francis St.
Boston, MA 02115
(617) 732-5771
Director: Dr. Michael E. Charness

National Arts Medicine Center
National Rehabilitation Hospital
3 Bethesda Metro Ctr. Suite 950
Bethesda, MD 20814
(301) 654-9160
Director: Dr. Richard Norris

Instrumental Artists Hotline and Clinic
Sister Kenny Institute
800 E. 28th St.
Minneapolis, MN 55407
(612) 863-4495
Director: Dr. Jeanine Speier

Mayo Clinic
200 Second St.
Rochester, MN 55905
(507) 284-2511 X 7129
Contact: Dr. Ann Schutt

Medical Program for the Performing Arts
Jewish Hospital
216 S. Kingshighway
St. Louis, MO 63110
(314) 454-STAR
Director: Dr. Jerome Gilden

Neurologic Restoration Center
Bethesda Hospital
3655 Vista Ave.
St. Louis, MO 63110
(314) 776-8100
Director: Dr. Simon Horenstein

Dr. George Saari
925 Highland Blvd.
Bozeman, MT 59715
(406) 587-5533

Dr. Peter Stern
7615 Indian School Rd.
Albuquerque, NM 87110
(505) 883-6281

Department of Nuclear Medicine
105 Parker Hall
3435 Main St.
Buffalo, NY 14214
(716) 838-5889
Contact: Dr. Alan Lockwood

Neurological Consultants of Central New York
P. O. Box 505
5730 Commons Park
Dewitt, NY 13214
(315) 449-0011
Contact: Dr. Pieter Kark

Miller Institute for Performing Artists
St. Lukes/Roosevelt Hospital
425 W. 59th St.
New York, NY 10019
(212) 554-6314
Director: Dr. Emil Pascarelli

Institute of Rehabilitation Medicine
NYU School of Medicine
400 East 34th St.
New York, NY 10016
Contact: Dr. Matthew Lee

Roosevelt Hospital
Department of Hand Surgery
428 W. 59th St.
New York, NY 10019
(212) 523-7591
Contact: Dr. Richard Eaton

Shmuel Tatz Physical Therapy
Carnegie Hall Studio 142
154 W. 57th St.
New York, NY 10019
(212) 246-7308

Blythedale Children's Hospital
Department of Rehabilitation Medicine
Valhalla, NY 10595
(914) 592-7555
Contact: Dr. Yasoma Challenor

Dr. David Goode
3000 Bethesda Place, Suite 102
Winston-Salem, NC 27103-3323
(919) 760-0120

Clinic for the Performing Arts
2123 Auburn
Cincinnati, OH 45219
(513) 281-3224
Director: Dr. G. James Sammarco

Medical Center for Performing Artists
Cleveland Clinic Foundation
9500 Euclid Ave.
Cleveland, OH 44106
(216) 444-5545
Director: Dr. Richard Lederman

The Medical Center for Performing Artists
Suburban General Hospital
2705 Dekalb Pike
Norristown, PA 19401
(215) 279-1060
Director: Dr. David Rosenfeld

The Arts Medicine Center
1721 Pine St.
Philadelphia, PA 19103
(215) 928-8300
Director: Dr. Robert Sataloff

119

Dr. Robert G. Schwartz
Piedmont Physical Medicine and Rehabilitation
317 Francis Dr., Suite 350
Greenville, SC 29601

Dr. Paul Parsons
1345 Carters Creek Pike
Franklin, TN 37064
(615) 790-3290

The Southwest Regional Arts Medicine Center
The Institute for Rehabilitation and Research
Texas Medical Center
1333 Moursund Ave.
Houston, TX 77030-3405
(713) 799-5010; (800)-44REHAB
Director: Dr. Rebecca R. Clearman

The Clinic for Performing Artists
Section of Physical Medicine and Rehabilitation
Virginia Mason Medical Center
1100 Ninth Ave.
P. O. Box 900
Seattle, WA 98111
(206) 223-6600
Contact: Dr. Michael Weinstein

Performing Artists' Health Program
Centre for Human Performance and Health Promotion
Sir William Osler Health Institute
565 Sanatorium Rd.
Hamilton, Ontario L9C 7N4
Canada
(416) 574-5444
Director: Dr. John Chong

ISSTIP/London College of Music Performing Arts Clinic
London College of Music
Greater Marlborough St.
London, England W1V
Consultant: Dr. C. B. Wynn Parry

Dr. Jochen Blum
Am Rosengarten 5
D-6500 Mainz
Germany
(011) 49-6131-839-482

Music Medicine Clinic
The Conservatory of Bari
Bari, Italy
Director: Professor Alfredo Musajo-Somma, University of Bari
(for info: S. Edith Nicoletti, Via dei Chiavari 6, 00186 Roma,
Italy 686-7957)

Appendix C

Arts Medicine Organizations And Publications

Organizations

International Arts Medicine Association (IAMA)
3600 Market St.
Philadelphia, PA,19104
Rick Lippin, MD, President

Open membership, broadly based with emphasis on arts medicine information dissemination. Includes music and art therapy, humanizing effect of the arts (including poetry) on medical training. International liaisons.

Benefits of Membership: quarterly newsletter, *International Journal of Arts Medicine*

Performing Arts Medicine Association (PAMA)
Richard J. Lederman, MD, PhD, President
Department of Neurology
The Cleveland Clinic
9500 Euclid Avenue
Cleveland, OH 44195-5527

Membership open to non-physicians, physicians, resident physicians, physical therapists, and medical students. Yearly meeting in conjunction with Cleveland Clinic's Annual Symposium on the Medical Problems of Musicians and Dancers in Aspen, CO (concurrent with the Aspen Music Festival).

Benefits of membership: Journal *Medical Problems of Performing Artists*, occasional newsletter.

Publications

International Journal of Arts Medicine
Rosalie Rebollo Pratt, Editor
Publisher: MMB Music, Inc.
10370 Page Industrial Blvd.
St. Louis, MO 63132

Medical Problems of Performing Artists (Quarterly)
Alice Brandfonbrener, MD, Editor
Hanley and Belfus, Publishers
POB 1377
Philadelphia, PA 19105-9990

Arts Hazards News
Center for Safety in the Arts
5 Beekman St.
New York, NY 10038

Performing Arts Health News
Performing Arts Health Network
P.O. Box 566
New York, NY 10101-0566

Bibliography

This list is excerpted from bibliographies compiled by Susan Harman and is reprinted by permission. It focuses on the health problems of instrumental musicians. The list is mostly confined to the English language. Citations from the medical, musical, and popular literature have been included. The compiler attempts to provide citations which are as complete and correct as possible. The bibliography is periodically updated, but the compiler makes no claim of total comprehensiveness. A version of this bibliography appeared in the Dec. 1987 issue of *Medical Problems of Performing Artists*; periodic updates are planned.

Susan E. Harman, Associate Librarian, Clearinghouse Coordinator
Music Medicine Clearinghouse
Medical & Chirurgical Faculty Library
1211 Cathedral St.
Baltimore, Md. 21201
(410) 539-0872

Abram B. Musical tension and muscular ease. *Clavier* 1984 Jul-Aug; 23(6): 28-29.

Amadio PC; Russoti GM. Evaluation and treatment of hand and wrist disorders in musicians. *Hand Clinics* 1990 Aug; 6(3): 405-16.

An K; Bejjani FJ. Analysis of upper-extremity performance in athletes and musicians. *Hand Clinics* 1990 Aug; 6(3): 393-403.

Baird CM. A pianist's techniques of rehabilitation. *Medical Problems of Performing Artists* 1986 Dec; 1(4): 128-30.

Bejjani FJ; Stuchin S; Winchester R. Effect of joint laxity on musicians' occupational disorders. *Clinical Research* 1984; 32(2): 660A.

Bejjani FJ; Ferrara L; Xu N; Tomaino CM; Pavlidis L; Wu J; Dommerholt J. Comparison of three piano techniques as an implementation of a proposed experimental design. *Medical Problems of Performing Artists* 1989 Sep; 4(3): 109-13.

Berger KW. Respiratory and articulatory factors in wind instrument performance. *Journal of Applied Physiology* 1965 Nov; 20(6): 1217-21.

Bird H. Overuse injuries in musicians. *British Medical Journal* 1989 Apr 29; 298(6681): 1129-30.

Blum J; Ritter G. Violinists and violists with masses under the left side angle of the jaw known as "fiddler's neck." *Medical Problems of Performing Artists* 1990 Dec; 5(4): 155-60.

Bolomey W. Flute fitness II: potential problems of flutists: preventing or alleviating back and shoulder problems. *National Flute Association Newsletter* 1983 Winter; 8(2): 9.

Bosanquet RC. The Alexander principle and its importance to music education. *British Journal of Music Education* 1987; 4(3): 229-42.

Brandfonbrener AG. Beta blockers in the treatment of performance anxiety. *Medical Problems of Performing Artists* 1990 Mar; 5(1): 23-26.

Brandfonbrener AG. The epidemiology and prevention of hand and wrist injuries in performing artists. *Hand Clinics* 1990 Aug; 6(3): 365-77.

Brevig P. Losing one's lip and other problems of the embouchure. *Medical Problems of Performing Artists* 1991 Sep; 6(3): 105-7.

Bryant GWT. Myofascial pain dysfunction and viola playing. *British Dental Journal* 1989 May 6; 166(9): 335-36.

Cailliet R. Abnormalities of the sitting postures of musicians. *Medical Problems of Performing Artists* 1990 Dec; 5(4): 131-35.

Caldron P; Calabrese L; Lederman R; Clough J; Stulberg B; Bergfeld J. A survey of musculoskeletal problems encountered in high level musicians. *Arthritis and Rheumatism* 1985 Apr; 28(suppl 4): S97.

Charness ME; Barbaro NM; Olney RK; Parry GJ. Occupational cubital tunnel syndrome in instrumental musicians. *Neurology* 1987 Mar; 37(3 suppl 1): 115.

Charness ME; Parry GJ; Markison RE; Rosegay H; Barbaro NM. Entrapment neuropathies in musicians. *Neurology* 1985 Apr; 35(4 suppl 1): 74.

Clinch P. In support of Dr. Fry: overuse syndrome. *The Clarinet* 1987 Spring; 14(3): 51.

Cockey L; Gimble J; Joseph A. A teaching strategy for healthier performance: a practical guide for all music teachers. *American Music Teacher* 1989 Jan; 22-23, 65.

Cole RA; Cohen LG; Hallet M. Treatment of musician's cramp with botulinum toxin. *Medical Problems of Performing Artists* 1992 Dec; 6(4): 137-43.

Cutietta R. Biofeedback training in music: from experimental to clinical applications. *Council for Research in Music Education Bulletin* 1986 Spring; 87: 35-42.

Cynamon KB. Flutist's neuropathy. [letter] *New England Journal of Medicine* 1981 Oct 15; 305(16): 961.

Dawson WJ. Hand and upper extremity problems in musicians: epidemiology and diagnosis. *Medical Problems of Performing Artists* 1988 Mar; 3(1): 19-22.

Dawson WJ. Upper extremity injuries in high-level instrumentalists: an end-result study. *Medical Problems of Performing Artists* 1990 Sep; 5(3): 109-112.

Farkas P. Medical problems of wind players: a musician's perspective. *Cleveland Clinic Quarterly* 1986 Spring; 53(1): 33-37.

Faulkner M. Experimentation in breathing as it relates to brass performance. *Instrumentalist* 1967 Feb; 21(2): 6-7.

Feldenkrais M. *Awareness Through Movement: Health Exercises for Personal Growth*. New York: Harper & Row, 1977.

Fishbein M; Middlestadt SE; Ottai V; Straus S; Ellis A. Medical problems among ICSOM musicians: overview of a national survey. *Medical Problems of Performing Artists* 1988 Mar; 3(1): 1-8.

Flesch C. *The Art of Violin Playing*. 2d rev. ed. Eng. text Frederick H. Martens. New York: Carl Fischer, 1939.

Fray DL. Physiological studies in string playing. *American String Teacher* 1981 Winter; 31: 33-36.

Fry HJH. How to treat overuse injury: medicine for your practice. *Music Educators Journal* 1986 May; 72(9): 46-49.

Fry HJH. Incidence of overuse syndrome in the symphony orchestra. *Medical Problems of Performing Artists* 1986 Jun; 1(2): 51-55.

Fry HJH. Overuse injury at music school: the dilemma. *American Music Teacher* 1986 Feb-Mar; 36(4): 45.

Fry HJH. Overuse syndrome, alias tenosynovitis/tendinitis: the terminological hoax. *Plastic and Reconstructive Surgery* 1986 Sep; 78(3): 414-17.

Fry HJH. Overuse syndrome in musicians—100 years ago. An historical review. *Medical Journal of Australia* 1986 Dec 1-15; 145(11-12): 620-25.

Fry HJH. The effect of overuse on the musician's technique: a comparative and historical review. *International Journal of Arts Medicine* 1991 Fall; 1(1): 46-55.

Fry HJH; Peters G. Occupation-related physical problems of conductors: a study of 68 conductors. *Journal of the Conductors' Guild* 1987 Spring-Summer; 8(2-3): 93-95.

Gehrig RE. *Famous Pianists and Their Technique*. Washington, D.C.: Luce, 1974.

Goldstein LJ. When violin scars jaw, try custom chin rest. *Dental Survey* 1968 Sep; 44(9): 48-49.

Harding DC; Brandt KD; Hillberry BM. Minimization of finger joint forces and tendon tensions in pianists. *Medical Problems of Performing Artists* 1989 Sep; 4(3): 103-8.

Harman SE. Bibliography for occupational diseases of instrumental musicians— update. *Medical Problems of Performing Artists* 1988 Dec; 3(4): 163-65.

Harman SE. Bibliography for occupational diseases of instrumental musicians. *Medical Problems of Performing Artists* 1987 Dec; 2(4): 155-62.

Heggie J; Rose E. Awareness through movement. *Instrumentalist* 1986 Apr; 40: 36-39.

Hiner SL. Performance-related medical problems among premier violinists. *Medical Problems of Performing Artists* 1987 Jun; (2): 67-71.

Hirsch JA; McCall WD Jr; Bishop B. Jaw dysfunction in viola and violin players. *Journal of the American Dental Association* 1982 Jun; 104(6): 838-43.

Hochberg FH; Leffert RD; Heller MD; Merriman L. Hand difficulties among musicians. *Journal of the American Medical Association* 1983 Apr 8; 249(14): 1869-72.

Hochberg FH; Harris SU; Blattert TR. Occupational hand cramps: professional disorders of motor control. *Hand Clinics* 1990 Aug; 6(3): 417-28.

Horvath J. Playing hurt. *Duet* 1990 Apr: 16.

Hotchkiss RN. Common disorders of the elbow in athletes and musicians. *Hand Clinics* 1990 Aug; 6(3): 507-15.

Howard JA; Lovrovich AT. Wind instruments: their interplay with orofacial structures. *Medical Problems of Performing Artists* 1989 Jun; 4(2): 59-72.

Jones F. *Body Awareness in Action: a Study of the Alexander Technique.* New York: Schocken, 1979.

Kella JJ. A guide to preventing musicians' occupational injuries. *Allegro* 1989 Apr; 89(4): 13, 15, 19.

Knishkowy B; Lederman RJ. Instrumental musicians with upper extremity disorders: a follow-up study. *Medical Problems of Performing Artists* 1986 Sep; 1(3): 85-89.

Kochevitsky G. The physiology of speed in piano playing. *American Music Teacher* 1972 Nov-Dec; 22(2): 32-34.

Krivin M; Congorth SG. An embouchure aid for clarinet and saxophone players. *Journal of the American Dental Association* 1975 June; 90: 1277-81.

Lascelles RG; Mohr PD; Neary D; Bloor K. The thoracic outlet syndrome. *Brain* 1977 Sep; 100(3): 601-12.

Lederman RJ. Focal dystonia in instrumentalists: clinical features. *Medical Problems of Performing Artists* 1991 Dec; 6(4): 132-36.

Lederman RJ. Nerve entrapment syndromes in instrumental musicians. *Medical Problems of Performing Artists* 1986 Jun; 1(2): 45-48.

Lederman RJ. Peripheral nerve disorders in instrumentalists. *Annals of Neurology* 1989 Nov; 26(5): 640-46.

Lederman RJ. Thoracic outlet syndromes: review of the controversies and a report of 17 instrumental musicians. *Medical Problems of Performing Artists* 1987 Sep; 2(3): 87-91.

Levee JR. Electromyographic biofeedback for relief of tension in the facial and throat muscles of a woodwind musician. *Biofeedback and Self-Regulation* 1976; 1(1): 113-20.

LeVine WR; Irvine JK. In vivo EMG biofeedback in violin and viola pedagogy. *Biofeedback and Self-Regulation* 1984 Jun; 9(2): 161-68.

Lieberman JL. You are your instrument: muscular challenges in practice and performance. *Strings* 1989 Nov-Dec: 48-50.

Lockwood AH. Medical problems in secondary school-aged musicians. *Medical Problems of Performing Artists* 1988 Dec; 3(4): 129-32.

Lockwood AH. Medical problems of musicians. *New England Journal of Medicine* 1989 Jan 26; 320(4): 221-27.

Maffulli N; Maffulli F. Transient entrapment neuropathy of the posterior interosseous nerve in violin players. *Journal of Neurology Neurosurgery and Psychiatry* 1991 Jan; 54(1): 65-67.

Marion JD; Sheppard JE. An orthotic device to prevent thumb joint hyperextension following carpometacarpal arthritis surgery: a case study. *Medical Problems of Performing Artists* 1991 Sep; 6(3): 90-92.

Markison RE. Treatment of musical hands: redesign of the interface. *Hand Clinics* 1990 Aug; 6(3): 525-44.

Meador R. The treatment of shoulder pain and dysfunction in a professional viola player: implications of the latissimus dorsi and teres major muscles. *Journal of Orthopaedic and Sports Physical Therapy* 1989 Aug; 11(2): 52-55.

Middlestadt SE; Fishbein M. The prevalence of severe musculoskeletal problems among male and female symphony orchestra string players. *Medical Problems of Performing Artists* 1989 Mar; 4(1): 41-48.

Murray A. The Alexander technique. *Medical Problems of Performing Artists* 1986 Dec; 1(4): 131-33.

Nagel JJ. Performance anxiety and the performing musician: a fear of failure or a fear of success? *Medical Problems of Performing Artists* 1990 Mar; 5(1): 37-40.

Nelson SH. Playing with the entire self: the Feldenkrais method and musicians. *Seminars in Neurology* 1989 Jun; 9(2): 97-104.

Newmark J; Lederman RJ. Practice doesn't necessarily make perfect: incidence of overuse syndromes in amateur instrumentalists. *Medical Problems of Performing Artists* 1987 Dec; 2(4): 142-44.

Nolan WB; Eaton RG. Thumb problems of professional musicians. *Medical Problems of Performing Artists* 1989 Mar; 4(1): 20-24.

Norris R. Fit as a fiddle: taking care of the person behind the musical instrument. *Senza Sordino* 1991 Jun-Aug; 29(5-6): 4-5.

Norris RN. Applied ergonomics: the angled-head flute. *Flutist Quarterly* 1989 Summer; 14(3): 60-61.

Norris RN. Seating problems of flutists. *Flutist Quarterly* 1991 Spring; 16(2): 11-13.

Pierce A; Pierce R. Pain and healing: for pianists part 2. *Piano Quarterly* 1983; 31(122): 38-39.

Pierce A; Pierce R. Pain and healing: for pianists—part 3. *Piano Quarterly* 1984; 32(126): 45-49.

Pierce A; Pierce R. Pain and healing: for pianists. *Piano Quarterly* 1982; 30(118): 43-47.

Polnauer FF. *Total Body Technique of Violin Playing.* Bryn Mawr, Pa.: Theodore Presser, 1974.

Porter MM. Dental problems in wind instrument playing. 1. Dental aspects of embouchure. *British Dental Journal* 1967 Oct 17; 123: 393-96.

Revak JM. Incidence of upper extremity discomfort among piano students. *American Journal of Occupational Therapy* 1989 Mar; 43(3): 149-54.

Reynolds C; Morasky R. Intensity without tension: biofeedback. *Music Educators Journal* 1981 Mar; 67(9): 53-55.

Rolland P. Arm balance: a critical element of efficient bow and vibrato technique. *Strad* 1970; 81: 25, 27, 29, 31, 63, 65, 67.

Sataloff RT; Brandfonbrener AG; Lederman RJ. *Textbook of Performing Arts Medicine.* New York: Raven Press, 1990.

Schneider A. Dorothy Taubman: there is an answer. *Clavier* 1983 Sep; 22(7): 19-21.

Scott J. Functions of the throat in wind playing: new views. *Flutist Quarterly* 1988 Spring; 13(2): 44-48.

Singer K. *Diseases of the Musical Profession: A Systematic Presentation of their Causes, Symptoms and Methods of Treatment.* tr W. Lakond. New York: Greenberg, 1932.

Solow J. Physically efficient string playing. *Seminars in Neurology* 1989 Jun; 9(2): 119-21.

Spaulding C. Before pathology: prevention for performing artists. *Medical Problems of Performing Artists* 1988 Dec; 3(4): 135-39.

Spire M. The Feldenkrais method: an interview with Anat Baniel. *Medical Problems of Performing Artists* 1989 Dec; 4(4): 159-62.

Stern PJ. Tendinitis, overuse syndrome, and tendon injuries. *Hand Clinics* 1990 Aug; 6(3): 467-76.

Sternbach D. Taking control of your stress—on stage and off. *International Musician* 1988 Aug; 87(2): 9, 21.

Tubiana R. Movements of the fingers. *Medical Problems of Performing Artists* 1988 Dec; 3(4): 123-28.

Tubiana R; Champagne P. Functional anatomy of the hand. *Medical Problems of Performing Artists* 1988 Sep; 3(3): 83-87.

Tubiana R; Champagne P; Brockman R. Fundamental positions for instrumental musicians. *Medical Problems of Performing Artists* 1989 Jun; 4(2): 73-76.

Wainapel SF; Cole JL. The not-so-magic flute: two cases of distal ulnar nerve entrapment. *Medical Problems of Performing Artists* 1988 June; 3(2): 63-65.

White ER; Basmajian JV. Electromyography of lip muscles and their role in trumpet playing. *Journal of Applied Physiology* 1973 Dec; 35(6): 892-97.

Wilson FR. Fernando Laires and Dorothy Taubman talk with Dr. Frank Wilson about Isidor Philipp and his "exercises." *Piano Quarterly* 1987 Summer; 138: 36-39.

Wilson FR. Mind, Muscle and Music: Physiological Clues to Better Teaching. *Teachercraft Bulletin* no. 4. Elkhart, In: Selmer, 1981.

Wilson FR. Teaching hands, treating hands. *Piano Quarterly* 1988; 36(141): 34-36, 38-41.

Wolff K. Dorothy Taubman: the pianist's medicine woman. *Piano Quarterly* 1986 Spring; 34(133): 25-32.

About the National Arts Medicine Center

The National Arts Medicine Center is part of the National Rehabilitation Hospital (NRH) in Washington, D.C. Open since July 1992, it is situated in a new facility at Three Bethesda Metro Center in Bethesda, Maryland, separate from the main hospital campus. The 15,000-square-foot facility also houses NRH's new Back Rehabilitation Program and the Center for Repetitive Motion Disorders.

The National Arts Medicine Center's interdisciplinary staff includes specially trained physicians, physical therapists, and psychologists, led by medical director Richard N. Norris, M.D., a specialist in physical medicine and rehabilitation. Dr. Norris, a leading figure in the field of arts medicine, was recruited from Boston by NRH to develop and establish this new program.

The National Arts Medicine Center serves musicians, dancers, theater artists, and visual artists from the greater metropolitan Washington area, Virginia, Maryland, and much of the southeastern United States. The focus is on diagnosis and rehabilitation of neuromuscular and orthopedic disorders with medically designed and supervised treatment plans that allow artists to continue their professional activities in an active mode while undergoing treatment. On-site psychology services include treatment for performance anxiety and creative block, and support groups for injured artists. The Center features state-of-the-art equipment such as multichannel biofeedback with visual display for muscular re-education during practice and performance.

Video analysis for posture and technique assessment in dancers and musicians takes place in either a special room equipped with a dance floor, barre, and mirrors, or in our piano/music room.

Extensive back rehabilitation equipment from the Back Program is available as needed.

The Center has established health education programs for the arts community. Local leaders in the arts sit on an advisory board to help the Center to define and meet their needs. An anticipated collaboration with Very Special Arts will create an assistive technology program to enable persons with physical disabilities to participate actively in the arts.

For more information, contact:

Richard N. Norris, M.D.
Medical Director, National Arts Medicine Center
Three Bethesda Metro Center, Suite 950
Bethesda, MD 20814

Richard Norris, M.D.

Dr. Richard Norris is a leading figure in the new field of performing arts medicine, a medical discipline that addresses the diagnosis and rehabilitation of the occupational injuries of artists. His extensive background studying both music and dance provides Dr. Norris with an in-depth understanding of the unique needs and requirements of artists who are confronted with temporary disabilities. Indeed, he has been extremely successful in designing medically directed treatment plans that allow artists to continue their professional activities in an active mode while still undergoing medical treatment.

After graduating with honors from medical school in Guadalajara, Mexico, Dr. Norris completed his residency in physical medicine and rehabilitation at St. Vincent's Hospital in New York City. He served a fellowship in pediatric orthopedics at Harvard University's Boston Children's Hospital. Subsequently, he served a second fellowship in pediatric rehabilitation at the Albert Einstein College of Medicine in New York. Dr. Norris is both a Diplomate and a Fellow of the American Academy of Physical Medicine and Rehabilitation. He is also the founder and chairman of the Academy's Arts Medicine Special Interest Group.

Dr. Norris recently joined the medical staff of the National Rehabilitation Hospital in Washington, D.C., where he is medical director of the new National Arts Medicine Center. Prior to joining the NRH staff, he operated the highly acclaimed Boston Arts Medicine Center, the first facility of its kind in the greater New England area, and was a faculty member of the New England Conservatory of Music.

Dr. Norris is vice-president of the International Arts Medicine Association and is very active as both a member of the board of directors and chairman of the education committee of the Performing Arts Medicine Association. He is a faculty member of Catholic University's Rome School of Music, and serves as a medical consultant to the National Symphony Orchestra and the Washington Ballet.